THE ROOTS OF ALCOHOLICS ANONYMOUS

BILL PITTMAN

Foreword by
Daniel J. Anderson, Ph.D.
President Emeritus, Hazelden Foundation

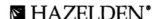

Hazelden
Center City, Minnesota 55012-0176

1-800-328-9000
1-651-213-4590 (Fax)
www.hazelden.org

©1988 by Bill Pittman

First published by Glen Abbey Books 1988 (originally titled *A.A.: The Way It Began*). First published by Hazelden Foundation 1999
All rights reserved. Printed in the United States of America
No portion of this publication may be reproduced in any manner without the written permission of the publisher

ISBN: 1-56838-505-6

03   6 5 4 3

Editor's note:
 The publication of this volume does not imply affiliation with nor approval or endorsement from Alcoholics Anonymous World Services, Inc.

Hazelden Publishing and Educational Services is a division of the Hazelden Foundation, a not-for-profit organization. Since 1949, Hazelden has been a leader in promoting the dignity and treatment of people afflicted with the disease of chemical dependency.

The mission of the foundation is to improve the quality of life for individuals, families, and communities by providing a national continuum of information, education, and recovery services that are widely accessible; to advance the field through research and training; and to improve our quality and effectiveness through continuous improvement and innovation.

Stemming from that, the mission of this division is to provide quality information and support to people wherever they may be in their personal journey—from education and early intervention, through treatment and recovery, to personal and spiritual growth.

Although our treatment programs do not necessarily use everything Hazelden publishes, our bibliotherapeutic materials support our mission and the Twelve Step philosophy upon which it is based. We encourage your comments and feedback.

The headquarters of the Hazelden Foundation is in Center City, Minnesota. Additional treatment facilities are located in Chicago, Illinois; New York, New York; Plymouth, Minnesota; St. Paul, Minnesota; and West Palm Beach, Florida. At these sites, we provide a continuum of care for men and women of all ages. Our Plymouth facility is designed specifically for youth and families.

For more information on Hazelden, please call **1-800-257-7800.** Or you may access our World Wide Web site on the Internet at **www.hazelden.org.**

This book is gratefully dedicated to

Patrick Butler

FOREWORD

The Roots of Alcoholics Anonymous is a careful, well-documented history of the original sources of knowledge, inspiration, and wisdom developed by the early members of Alcoholics Anonymous. Over time and through experience, these important ingredients were forged into the basic, now traditional principles and practices that constitute the Fellowship of AA.

Author Bill Pittman's attention to detail and obvious caring and sensitivity to the material have brought that history alive. *The Roots of Alcoholics Anonymous* is a significant contribution to the literature on this exciting subject. It is a much needed and very readable accounting of the remarkable organization known as AA. I am quite confident that AA members throughout the country will find this history very interesting, for their groups and as individuals.

Daniel J. Anderson, Ph.D.
President Emeritus
Hazelden Foundation

PREFACE

The modern conception of alcoholism as a disease actually dates back to the late 1700s. During approximately the next 200 years, alcoholism was dealt with in a variety of ways. Whether alcoholism is a disease or merely "drinking more alcohol than others think you should" will not be argued in the pages of this book. It is the contention of this work that efforts used to deal with alcohol in the past have dramatically and dynamically influenced our present attitudes. As an example, does 18th century thoughts on American temperance have any relevance today?

An outline of American ideas, treatments and movements dealing with alcohol use and misuse will be discussed in the pages to follow, and will focus especially on the 1890s. This presentation will hopefully provide a background for an understanding of the founding of Alcoholics Anonymous in the 1930s. This history will concentrate on the life of Bill Wilson (1895 - 1971), co-founder of AA, prior to and including the publication of the book Alcoholics Anonymous in 1939, (also referred to as the "Big Book") the "bible" of this therapeutic social movement.

Although any attempt to write this history must rely on conflicting interpretations, (as self-reports are usually not complete and tend to conflict) it is the intention of this analysis to add information on the history of AA to the present literature.

This work (formerly titled "Alternative Explanations For the Beginnings of Alcoholics Anonymous, 1934 - 1939") was originally written as partial fulfillment for my Bachelor of Science degree summa cum laude, Major Alcohol Studies and Alcoholism Counseling, University of Minnesota, June 1983. The comments of two friends, Nell Wing and Ernest Kurtz, Ph.D., have helped in the revision of this work, although interpretations, opinions and conclusions expressed herein are the responsibility of the author. My hope is that this book will not only be of interest to persons in the Alcohol Studies Field, but also to members of Alcoholics Anonymous.

ACKNOWLEDGMENTS

I wish to express my gratitude to the individuals whose encouragement and support allowed me to begin and complete this work: Dan Anderson, Ph.D., Leonard Blumberg, Ph.D., Bruce Carruth, Ph.D., Eli Coleman, Ph.D., Gordon Grimm, Ernest Kurtz, Ph.D., Mark Lender, Ph.D., and Damian McElrath, Ph.D, Penny Page, and Sharon Woods, M.D. And a note of appreciation to the members of my summa cum laude committee at the University of Minnesota at Minneapolis: Paul Cashman, Ph.D., Marjorie Cowmeadow, Ph.D., Bruce Fisher, M.A., William Goodman, Ph.D., Jim Rothenberger, M.Ph.

My thanks to the following individuals who allowed me, through written and oral communications, to obtain an historical perspective of Alcoholics Anonymous: Ruth Hock Crecelius, Irving Harris, Mark Keller, Barry Leach, Helen Shoemaker, Clarence Snyder, Lois Wilson, and Nell Wing.

Also, a special thank you to Ann Cordillia, Ph.D., Robert Dentler, Ph.D., Gerald Garrett, Ph.D., Karen O'Jenos, M.A., Colleen Price-Rys, M.A., and Rita Siragusa, M.A. at the University of Massachussets at Boston and John Dodd, Sheryl Feldinger, M.A., Herbert Menzel, Ph.D. and Erika Segall at New York University for their assistance in my educational progress.

A special acknowledgment and thanks to the following individuals who have helped me with my writing, academic endeavors, and personal journey: Lee Asselta, Charles B., Franklin B., Pete B., Ed Brady, Judy C., Lillian D., Fred, Helen and Steve Dahlin, Norman Denzin, Ph.D., Lee Dean, Joan Frederickson, Dale Fuqua, Retha G., Dorothy G., Fran H., Barry and Heidi Herman, Maritza Hernandez, Joan Jackson, Ph.D., Margie Janicek, Eurdora and Joe Jenkins, Orv L., Tom and Mary Beth Legeros, Regina and Peter L., Frank M., Don Meurer, Curtis and Wendy M., Bill Mc K., Bob M., Gerrie M., Jose Natal, Gail N., Ciarán O'Mahony, Tony Osnato, Brad, Matt, Mark, Nancy, Marilyn, and Randi Pittman, Wayne P., Susan and Erik U., Julie R., Charles S., Naomi Strassberg, Ames S., Harold A. Swift, A.C.S.W., Marcia T., Helen T., Albert Waldman, M.D., Ann W., Eleanor W., and a special note of gratitude for his friendship and inspiration, Paz Daly.

Table of Contents

Foreword vi
Preface vii
Acknowledgements ix
BRIEF HISTORY OF ALCOHOL AND ALCOHOLISM 1
CAUSES OF ALCOHOLISM 11
CLASSIFICATION OF ALCOHOLICS 19
ALCOHOLISM TREATMENTS In The 1890s . 26
   Penal and Punitive Treatments for Alcoholism 27
   Institutional Treatment 34
   Mental Treatments and Hypnotism 49
   Temperance Societies 55
   Drug Cures 57
   Immunological and Serum Treatments 61
   Health and Nutritional Cures 63
   Radical Treatments 65
   Quack Cures 67
   Religious Conversion Cure 72
THE "PROHIBITION CURE" 82
   Charles B. Towns 83
   The Emmanuel Movement and Peabodyism . . 87
   <u>Religion and Medicine</u> (1908) 88
   <u>Mind, Religion and Health</u> (1909) 91

Remaking A Man (1919) 93
  The Common Sense of Drinking (1930) . . . 101
  Body, Mind, and Spirit (1931) 109
THE OXFORD GROUP 113
  Special Techniques of the Oxford Group . . . 123
WILLIAM GRIFFITH WILSON AND
    ALCOHOLICS ANONYMOUS 132
  Vermont 132
  Bennington County and Dorset, Vermont . . 134
  William Griffith Wilson (1895-1939) 136
WILLIAM GRIFFITH WILSON, 1934-1939 . . 162
  The "Hot Flash" 162
  William James and The Varieties of Religious
      Experience 170
  The Oxford Group 174
  Writing of the "Big Book" 179
  Books Early AAs Found Helpful 182
SUMMARY, CONCLUSIONS, AND
RECOMMENDATIONS 184
  Summary 184
  Conclusions 185
  Chronological Chart of Precursors to AA . . . 187
  Recommendations 188
APPENDICES
  A References Suggested in Peabody's Book . . 190

- B Nell Wing's List of Books
    Early AAs Read 192
- C Sam Shoemaker Books 193
- D Books Written by Oxford
    Group Members 194
- E Books Critical of Oxford Group 196
- F Dr. Bob's Required Reading List 197
- G The AA Preamble, Steps and
    Traditions 197
- H Additional Information for AA
    and Al-Anon 205

LIST OF REFERENCES 206

INDEX 231

Chapter One

BRIEF HISTORY OF ALCOHOL AND ALCOHOLISM

Alcohol and the effects of alcohol consumption have long been known to civilized man, but since the beginning, along with the use of alcoholic beverages for religious and medicinal purposes, there has been a corresponding abuse of alcohol consumption. Such abuse was common among the Egyptians, who had regulations providing for the flogging and imprisoning of drunkards. The Greeks had their Bacchanalian rites, firmly established by 600 B.C., and the Romans celebrated both the Floralia, which lasted from mid-April through May, and the Saturnalia, a December festival. The drunkenness of those celebrating was noted by both Galen (<u>Compositions of Medicines</u>) and Pliny (Books XX, XXI, XXX, C5, XXXII, C10); they also described some of the more common treatments. [1] These were generally of three types.

First, there were the preventatives; spices, honey, ginger, cheese, sea water, resins, or vinegar were added to wine in an effort to prevent the spirits from entering the head and causing intoxication. Some revelers wore special wreaths, crowns, and dresses in an effort to ward off the effects of drinking. The second type of treatment was used to ease the after-effects of a drinking bout; cabbage, various bitters, laxatives and diuretics, herbs, and "hair of the dog" treatments, which consisted of more alcohol of certain specified kinds. Finally, there were legal and punitive measures, instituted at various times by the Greeks, the Romans, who for a short time had a death sentence for any noble found intoxicated, the Christians, and the Turks (whose Koran recommended pouring molten lead down the drunkard's throat). (3; 4)

Alcoholism as a disease was seldom described in the ancient world, although Seneca and Pliny described the effects of chronic indulgence. Seneca maintained that the word "drunken" refers to two situations: to that of a man who is loaded with wine and has no control of himself; and to that of a man who is accustomed to getting drunk and is a slave to the habit. (2)

What do the Scriptures tell us in regard to wine? The term wine is variously applied in the Bible to the juice of the grape, fermented and unfermented, intoxicating and unintoxicating.

> There are two modes of interpreting Scripture references to wine. By the one mode, our divine Master made, and the Bible sanctioned, the social use of wine containing poison in an intoxicating proportion. By the other mode, the wine the Bible condemns is the wine with poisoning properties; while the wine, the moderate use of which the Bible approves, and which our Saviour made, was not poisonous, but wholesome. (6)

Besides its ceremonial, religious, and medicinal usages, wine also takes on a particular divine blessing so widely recognized in the Old and New

Testaments that it has influenced our American culture. (5)

The Bible also records divine commands to abstain: to Aaron and his sons, to John the Baptist, to Samson, to the Rechabites, and so on. It teaches that abstinence is in accordance with health, as in the case of Daniel, and contains warnings against habitual drinking and even drinking at all (Prov. XXXIII:31). (7) This aspect of how the Bible views the use of spirits was to have a great impact on the Temperance Movement in America.

The law of St. Gildas, enacted at the end of the sixth century, sent monks too drunk to sing the psalmody to bed without supper. This law was an indication that drunkenness was becoming an important problem among the clergy. In the eighth century, St. Boniface, in a letter to the Archbishop of Canterbury, condemned drunkenness as a crime, especially for a member of the clergy. Very likely, he was commenting on several bishops of the Archbishop's diocese who were well known for their drunkenness and for encouraging others to get intoxicated.(8)

By the tenth century, Edgar, a Saxon king, had instituted a form of prohibition by reducing the number of alehouses allowed in the villages and, with the help of Dunstan, Archbishop of Canterbury, instituted the custom of "drinking to the peg." The large drinking cups then in use in the alehouses had a peg inserted and it became a penal offense to drink beyond the peg. During the reign of

Edward I, early closing, restricted hours on Sundays, and fines on poor quality beverages were instituted. The use of wine was also restricted to those of a certain social rank: only those who were above the rank of baron, made over one hundred marks in a year, or owned one thousand pounds of property could have more than ten gallons of wine in their possession during a year. Violators were fined.

In the late Middle Ages, the state of drinking and the number of drunkards can be inferred from the literature of the period, such as Chaucer's The Canterbury Tales, Gower's Confession Amantis, and Langland's Piers Plowman, all of which discuss drunkenness directly.

James I, in 1606, instituted laws for drunkenness whereby a person could be tried and convicted up to six months after the offense on the testimony of only one person. The choice of a fine or six hours in the stocks was normally given. Fines were also levied against those innkeepers who allowed tippling (to drink alcoholic beverages, especially habitually, to excess) and against those who ran unlicensed alehouses. [9] Again, offenders usually had a choice between a fine or a public whipping.

In addition to fines, many other methods of dealing with drunkards were common. People were subject to the stocks, the pound, and the pillory, where prisoners were used as targets by the jeering crowds; to dunking in filthy water; the Newcastle jacket (wearing a barrel); and the filthy hurdle (being dragged through cesspools). By the 1650s, the abusive treatment of drunkards had become more common, and in many cases, those who died as a result of drinking had their bodies either buried at a crossroads or burned.

At this point in our chronology of events, we travel across the Atlantic to America, along with the Pilgrims. They and other New World immigrants brought over European alcoholic beverages, drinking customs, and social attitudes. Many early settlers assumed that people drank and got drunk because they <u>wanted</u> to, not because they <u>had</u> to; also, that drunkenness was a natural, harmless consequence of drinking. (10) In 1673, Increase Mather published his sermon "Woe to Drunkards," deploring the frequency of excessive drinking in the Colonies. By 1712, the problem was even more widespread, and Increase's son, Cotton, preached to members of his congregation about drunkenness. By the 1760s, John Adams was so concerned about the level of drunkenness that he proposed limiting the number of taverns and Benjamin Franklin labeled taverns "a pest to society." Despite such complaints, however, and despite regulations on the amount of time one could spend in a tavern, how much one could drink there, and penalties for drunkenness, including public whippings and the stocks, Americans continued to drink and get drunk. (11)

The start of a modern way of viewing drunkards took place toward the end of the 1700s with the writings of two Philadelphians: "The Mighty Destroyer Displayed" (1774) by Quaker reformer Anthony

Benezet, and "Inquiry into the Effects of Ardent Spirits upon the Human Body and Mind" (1785) by Dr. Benjamin Rush. According to Rush, drunkards were "addicted" to spirituous liquor, and they became addicted gradually and progressively. Those who supposed that the American Medical Association discovered, in 1956, that alcoholism is a disease should note that Dr. Rush explicitly stated the same 171 years earlier.[5] He clearly described the drunkard's condition as loss of control over drinking behavior, declared the condition to be a disease, and prescribed total abstinence as the only way to cure a drunkard. [10] Dr. Rush was the first American medical authority on alcoholism.

Almost simultaneously in England, Dr. Thomas Trotter wrote a paper entitled "Essay, Medical, Philosophical and Chemical, on Drunkenness," which caused such a stir that he received the thanks of the Royal Humane Society for his work. His definition of alcoholism goes as follows:

> In medical language, I consider drunkenness, strictly speaking, to be a disease; produced by a remote cause, and giving birth to actions and movements in the living body, that disorder the functions of health. [12]

Between 1790 and 1830, Americans seem to have gone on an alcohol binge; the per capita consumption of distilled spirits rose dramatically as migration and social dislocation further dislodged traditional controls. At the same time, the New England Federalist elite began to worry about the spread of religious irreverence, democracy, and distilled alcohol. They countered it with religious revivalism and encouraged general temperance activity. The Connecticut Society for the Reformation of Morals and the Massachusetts Society for the Suppression of Intemperance (both founded in 1813) were formed and led by clergymen and laymen of wealth, prominence and Federalist politics. The first national temperance association, the American Temperance Society (founded in 1826), was led by Congregationalist and nonevangelical Presbyterian ministers with Federalist commitment, such as Jedidiah Morse. [14] The American Society for the Promotion of Temperance (ATS), "the crystallization of sober sentiment," was founded in New England in 1829.

At this time an important temperance reformer emerged, Lyman Beecher, author of <u>Six Sermons on Intemperance</u>, who began making a more direct attack on alcohol, calling for abstinence, not just temperance. [15] The temperance movement was a direct result of the increased interest, on the part of the general public, in the effects and results of alcohol consumption. When the American Temperance Society was founded and the temperance movement began to take hold, there were a thousand local societies with a claimed membership of a hundred thousand; by 1834 this had increased to five thousand local societies with a claimed membership of a million. At the same time, a drive was started to make more information available to the public and a temperance press for the publication and dissemination of pertinent information was started, along with a temperance newsletter. In 1836 the idea of temperance was altered to a position of total abstinence, rather than abstention just from distilled spirits. This new orientation caused a reduction in membership and the loss of some of the wealthier supporters.

The movement did little for the next four years, until the Washingtonian Movement. The Washington Temperance Society of Baltimore, active during the 1840s, is often compared with the Alcoholics Anonymous movement. After 1848 the temperance movements lost most of their momentum and ceased to be effective instruments of social change until the early part of the twentieth century.

Nineteenth century American temperance fiction acknowledged the progressive nature of alcoholism. In explaining the alcoholic process to the public, this fiction contributed to the general belief that the typical alcoholic was a skid row derelict. The most popular books included T.N. Soper's <u>Green Bluff</u>, L.M. Sargent's six volume <u>Temperance Tales</u>, and T.S. Arthur's <u>Strong Drink</u> and <u>Ten Nights in a Barroom</u>. A series of George Cruikshank prints, published in the 1850s to accompany a volume by T.S. Arthur detailed the fate of the James Latimer family after liquor entered their home and was typical of temperance art. [20]

During this period another movement began — the institutional treatment of alcoholics. In 1813, Thomas Sutton clearly defined and differentiated delirium tremens and prescribed for the syndrome.[13] In 1830 a committee of the Connecticut

Medical Society reported on the value of starting a special house devoted entirely to the treatment of alcoholics, but nothing was done at that time due to lack of funding. [16] The first home, in actuality simply a lodging house, was opened in 1845 by the Washington Total Abstinence Society. By 1850, interest in the society seems to have died down and nothing was heard of the home until 1858, when it reopened as the "Home for the Fallen." [17; 18] That same year Dr. Joseph Turner, in Binghamton, New York, advocated the formation of a home for the rehabilitation of alcoholics. Others started to become involved with the development of special institutions, and by 1868 three more homes for alcoholics had opened. [19]

Problems with alcoholism were not limited to the United States during the nineteenth century. By the early 1890s there was concern in most European countries about the increase of alcohol consumption. Reports appeared in most of the medical journals of the time; societies to investigate the causes and treatment of alcoholism existed in most major countries throughout the world and there were more than a hundred and fifty homes devoted entirely to the treatment of the alcoholic. Statistics on alcohol consumption during 1898 & 1900 cannot help but impress one. Tables 1 and 2 illustrate this point clearly; compare the quantities consumed per capita and note which, as will be described later, countries were having the most problems with alcohol abuse and which were the most advanced in their treatment programs. [3; 21]

Table 1
Alcohol Consumption Per Year in Liter/Person
(Debove, 1898)

Country	Liters/Person
Belgium	10.0
Germany	10.0
England	9.0
Switzerland	8.0
Italy	6.0
Sweden	4.0
Norway	3.0
Canada	2.0
Paris, France	14.5

Table 2
Consumption of Alcohol in Millions of Gallons
Per year, 1898
(Macfie, 1900)

Country	Wine	Beer	Spirits	Population*
Germany	71.412	1,353.396	100.364	56.400
France	838.000	199.122	71.895	39.000
UK	15.787	1,251.213	40.414	41.800
US (1898)	32.141	890.705	60.948	76.000
US (1960)	161.169	2,762.904	215.276	179.323

* In millions.

Chapter Two

CAUSES OF ALCOHOLISM

The idea that alcoholism could be a disease had been presented in the writings of Heroditus (ca. 500 B.C.), had extended through the Greek philosophers, and lasted for about two centuries into the Christian era. After that time and until the nineteenth century, alcoholism and the excessive use of alcohol were occasionally referred to as a disease, but usually were treated with punitive measures rather than medical means. During the 1800s, the idea that alcoholism could and should be thought of as a disease gained in popularity (i.e. Magnus Huss), although it was not without its opponents. The establishment, in 1870, of the American Association for the Study and Care of Inebriety was the first major step taken by an organized group to deal with alcoholism in medical rather than religious terms. [22] By 1893, the concept of alcoholism as a disease with an etiology, course, and definable symptoms, was well established. The treatment of alcoholism in all its stages was now under the domain of the medical profession, which began to examine the disease.

During the 1890s, one finds four major theories regarding the development of the disease "alcoholism." These theories can be roughly delineated as follows: first, alcohol is the cause of alcoholism; second, heredity is the determining factor in the development of alcoholism; third, precipitating factors are the key in development of the disease; and fourth, the environment a person is exposed to when young will determine whether or not a person becomes alcoholic. In addition, each implied a preferred course of treatment; these treatments will be dealt with.

The first and most easily understood of the theories is that alcohol is the determining cause of alcoholism. The logical deduction to be made from this theory is that a person who drinks to excess will become an alcoholic; if no one is allowed to drink, there will not be any alcoholics.

A corollary of this theory is that abstinence constitutes a cure for alcoholism and that to cure a person, all that needs to be done is to force abstinence in some way. One can gain the impression from the temperance societies of the time that alcoholism is more of a vice or bad habit that the drunkard is deliberately maintaining and that the disease consists of not being able to quit when forced to do so. [23; 24; 25; 26] In contrast, the second theory holds that heredity is the sole or main determining factor of alcoholism, and the alcoholic is unable to control whether or not he drinks. In its simplest form, the theory explains that a person who cannot control his drinking has inherited the condition from his parents and grandparents. The disease was thought both to have the tendency to skip generations at times and to be somewhat sex-linked; the sons of an alcoholic woman or the daughters of an alcoholic man were considered more likely to be affected than children of the same sex as the alcoholic parent.

Alcoholism was, at times, also viewed as a form of insanity, and there is frequent mention in the literature of a high degree of insanity, imbecility, epilepsy, and "moral degeneration" in the family of the alcoholic. There were those who held that if a person became an alcoholic through any cause, he would then pass on to his children a great deal of degeneracy in the form of physical, mental and intellectual defects. The issue of whether a parent can pass on acquired traits caused some confusion; one theory stated that the children of such a person who were born before the onset of alcoholism would be free of these defects, those born after would suffer from various defects. There was also discussion as to the effects of a parent being drunk at the time of a child's conception or during the nursing of the baby. (27;28;29)

By 1900, many of the fallacies of the heredity theory were pointed out by some of the more advanced people working in the physiology, treatment, and cure of alcoholism. Some started to adopt a hard-line approach to the treatment of the alcoholic by society and the treatment he expected to receive from the medical profession. They seemed to feel that by giving heredity a key role as the source of alcoholism, one was allowing the alcoholic to be freed of most of the responsibility for his drinking and his resulting behavior. This freedom was felt to be a detriment to the successful treatment of the alcoholic because it provided him with a rationalization for his drinking. (32; 33)

Critics of the heredity theory also felt that its proponents were misusing the field of genetics by claiming heredity as an all-purpose explanation and by not keeping separate the distinctions between variations and modifications. (34)

The third theory explains the development of alcoholism in terms of precipitating events in the environment. In many cases it was easy to find an event of major proportions on which the blame could be laid.

Trauma was postulated to be of two kinds, psychical and physical. Psychical trauma included any major emotional upheaval in a person's life - perhaps a financial setback or the death of a loved one. Any type of sudden development of alcoholism in a person for whom there was no physical cause or hereditary tendency toward the disease was thought to be psychical. Physical trauma was defined as any disease, injury or physical cause that brought on a sudden onset of alcoholism. Sunstroke, overexertion, nervous diseases, and blows on the head were some of the more common causes cited. (36)

Although there were some who held that a specific trauma could precipitate alcoholism, in most cases, the opinion was voiced that trauma could explain only a small number of the total alcoholic population. Another version of the theory was that most drinkers go through a specific pre-chronic stage in their drinking and unless there is a specific trauma, a drinker will not pass beyond this stage to become alcoholic. (22) The implication was that most people were equally susceptible to becoming alcoholics, but some just never had the chance or the proper circumstances. Most proponents of this theory believed that there was a probable hereditary disposition toward the development of alcoholism rather than some other form of illness. (37)

In line with the trauma theory was the belief that while a person many times had no control over whether or not he became an alcoholic, after alcoholism had developed it was within the ability of the person, at least until a large amount of physical damage had been done, to gain control of the disease and to help in the treatment procedure.

A factor considered by some to support the theory of traumatization was the "fact" that in most people alcoholism did not appear until the person was well into adulthood. The argument was put forth that if alcoholism was hereditary, there should be signs of it while a person was quite young; since most people who became alcoholics had been drinking for several years before they lost control of their drinking, some event must have caused them to lose control. However, when a consideration of alcoholism included France and Italy, one could not help but note the high incidence of alcoholism among children, including those of preschool age. This seems to be a definite argument against the viability of the trauma theory when applied to the general population of alcoholics. (35)

The fourth theory of the causes of alcoholism describes it as a result of the effects of environment on the young child. It was thought by proponents of this theory that most people become alcoholics through exposure to alcoholism while still young, either because of starting to drink at a very early age or having had at least one member of the household who was a problem drinker. (34; 36) Reid, (34) writing in 1899, conceded some influence of heredity in the etiology of alcoholism, but he felt that in general what most people claimed was the result of heredity was actually poisoning in the uterine environment or the influence of a bad home.

A correlate of this theory deals with the effects of the environment on a race's susceptibility to the effects of alcohol. The basic contention is that if alcoholism were allowed to exist and nothing done for those suffering from its ravages, the problem would soon cease to exist: those who had any tendency to alcoholism would develop the disease and die off. In this way, alcoholism would no longer be perpetuated. In his discussion of the theory, Reid (34) held that countries with established cultural ways of using alcohol and proscriptions against intemperance would soon become more temperate. Cultures that had long been exposed to alcohol would, as an extension of the theory, have the least problem with its abuse. As an example, he pointed to the temperate use of alcohol among the Jewish people. At the same time, a country that had never been exposed to the use of alcohol would become rapidly intemperate upon introduction of alcohol, because those who would be potentially susceptible to becoming alcoholics would rapidly develop the disease. As Wilson [33] points out, however, this theory does not explain alcoholism in people who have had neither a bad environment during childhood nor a hereditary predisposition to the development of dependencies. Nor did it deal with countries like France and Ireland, with large problems concerning alcoholism and a long history of alcohol use and production.

Several minor theories of the etiology of alcoholism were also current in the 1890s. The majority seem to be combinations of various points of the major theories. For example, a few people believed that alcoholism was caused by a gradual poisoning of the body until the person was no longer himself. At the point when a person lost control over his drinking, he became an alcoholic and could no longer be helped, since the alcohol had done irreparable damage.

Another theory, especially prevalent in France, held that alcohol, since it was such a good medicinal substance, could not possibly be the cause of alcoholism, or of all the damage normally traced to the consumption of alcohol. Accordingly, the element responsible for alcoholism was not alcohol, but the other impurities contained in beverages. [38] In Italy too, some theories were favorable to the idea that the impurities caused poisoning, and this poisoning mistakenly was called alcoholism. (21: 39)

Chapter Three

CLASSIFICATION OF ALCOHOLICS

The first step in all of the treatment programs of the 1890s was to ascertain what kind of a drunkard was being treated. Three different medical classification systems were in use: Avait's was the simplest and used mostly in France; Forel's system was in use in most of Germany; and Crothers' system was in use throughout most of the United States and Great Britain.

Marie Avait [44] assigned an alcoholic to one of three categories. The first was composed of simple drunks. These people were acute cases, occasional drunkards, and those who had suddenly and for no apparent reason started to drink. These people, she felt, could be the most easily and successfully treated of all alcoholics, especially if reached before the habit had firmly taken hold. The next category was composed of habitual drunkards: those who had been drinkers for a good length of time and for whom there was no ascertainable organic or hereditary cause for alcoholism. These people could be treated and cured only through much work and effort, usually requiring treatment of six months to two years. However, there was hope of a cure whenever the cooperation of the drinker could be enlisted. The final category was that of the incurable drinker. In this category one found the criminal drinker, the insane person, the congenital physical defective, and the mentally defective. The mentally defective subclass included those persons who had suffered intellectual impairment from defective genes, an injury, a disease or deterioration due to the consumption of alcohol for many years.

Mosel [45; 46] explained the categories in terms of those who could be helped by simple medical treatment, those who needed extended care but were still treatable, and those who were incurable and needed permanent institutionalization.

The classification of inebriates done in Germany usually followed the lines instituted in 1897 by Forel at Ellikon, a major home for the treatment of alcoholics. Forel divided alcoholics initially into curables and incurables. The curables were similar to the first two classes described by Avait, i.e., simple drinkers who could be controlled through the directions of a doctor and association with a temperance society, and also serious drinkers. Incurable drinkers were subdivided into five classes - chronic drinkers suffering physical damage, the alcoholic insane, drinking epileptics, delinquents, and hereditary alcoholics. For the curable alcoholics, unless there was extreme resistance from the patient, it was felt there was a good chance for improvement or cure. When dealing with the incurables, however, the most important decision made was on the type of institution in which the person was to be incarcerated.

As a subclass of curable drinkers, light drinkers or simple alcoholics were sometimes discussed as pre-alcoholic since they, with very simple means and much encouragement, could still gain control of their drinking. In contrast, serious drinkers, who had been under the influence of alcohol for many years, had more than likely sustained physical damage as a result and were not really amenable to any type of treatment procedures. Delirium tremens, often noted in this group of drinkers, caused enough manifestations of insanity that a serious drinker was re-classified as insane. Unlike the alcoholic psychotic, it was thought that there was still a chance for a cure in these cases.

The distinguishing characteristic between the chronic drinkers among the curables and those among the incurables was the amount of physical damage the person had sustained. When a person was no longer capable of making a "rational decision," he was classified among the incurables. The alcoholic insane were those in whom drinking was just another sign of their mental illness. The main problem with this group was not that they drank, but rather that they had little control over any of their behavior.

Believed to be equally incapable of abstinence were the epileptics, whose drinking was thought to be controlled by the same mechanism that produced their seizures. Although more care was being taken in the use of the designation "epileptic" one cannot help but speculate that any person who had ever had a seizure and later became an alcoholic was labeled epileptic.

Under the subgrouping of delinquent were all persons who either had committed a crime under the influence of alcohol or were thought to use alcohol as part of their "perversion."

The hereditary alcoholics were those who either had inherited general defects that prevented them from controlling their behavior or had seemingly inherited their alcoholism in the form of dipsomania. (47;48;49)

The system of classification most commonly used in the Untied States was that of Dr. T.D. Crothers. This system of classification was first developed and used in conjunction with the treatment programs advised by the American Association for the Study and Cure of Inebriety during the 1880s, and since then it had been widely adopted. (50; 51) Crothers first divided the alcoholic population into two main classes: inebriates and dipsomaniacs. The first class was then subdivided into four minor classes - accidental inebriates, emotional inebriates, solitary inebriates, and pauper inebriates. The major classification of dipsomania was broken down into subclasses of the acute, the periodic, and the chronic dipsomaniac. (22)

Inebriates constituted those whose disease was due to the influence of environment on the patient, either through direct action such as disease or injury, or through emotional strain such as financial loss or the death of a loved one.

The accidental inebriate's use of alcohol was totally dependent on external environment and conditions. People of this type would be model citizens in a temperate community, or the worst of drunkards where alcohol was freely available. Also in this class were those who developed a drinking problem through the medicinal use of alcohol.

Emotional inebriates were those who, being naturally unstable emotionally, had, through the use of alcohol for stabilization, become drunkards.

Solitary drinkers, those who drank only at night or alone, seemed to be very involved with keeping their drinking a secret. These people, according to Crothers, could often be important members of the community. Their drinking normally took a few more years than that of the other types of inebriates to get out of control.

Pauper inebriates were from the lower levels of society, perhaps constitutionally unable to keep their health and live in society. It was thought that inebriety was just another symptom of the general unfitness of this class to survive. Other conditions thought to be closely allied with inebriety in this class were criminality, pauperism, and prostitution.

Dipsomania, in contrast to inebriety, was a well defined disease. It was characterized by a sudden impulse to drink that would appear periodically, control the person, then relax its grip and leave the person completely free until the next bout. Acute dipsomania was rather uncommon; the drink impulse was thought to come on suddenly from the action of an external agent, such as sunstroke, overwork, or severe emotional strains.

Much more common was the periodic variety of dipsomania. In this class were the persons whose drinking was characterized by periodic attacks of drinking lasting for a definite length of time and alternating with sober spells. Many times there would be a noticeable change in the person's behavior just before the start of the spells. During this period, periodic dipsomania often was classified as a neurosis, as perhaps another form of epilepsy or hysteria.

Crothers, unlike some of the other doctors then working with alcoholics, considered the chronic dipsomania the most common form. People in this category generally had a long history of drinking, starting usually by the age of seventeen or eighteen and continuing from then on. Most were thought to have died by about age thirty, either from the direct effects of a drunken spree or from a functional disability brought on by overconsumption of alcohol. Chronic dipsomaniacs were similar to the periodic drinkers at the beginning, but soon lost control of their drinking; the temperate intervals disappeared and their life-style changed to one of fast living and a steady state of intoxication.

The prognosis for each of the classes of inebriates and dipsomaniacs was different, ranging from the accidental inebriate, whose drinking could be controlled by placing him in an environment in which he could not drink, to the chronic dipsomaniac, whose drinking was apparently uncontrollable. (22; 37;52)

A final category of alcoholics, not covered by any of the major classifications, was those who were chronic drinkers, with their drinking sometimes under control and sometimes not, who seemed to drink simply because they liked the taste of alcoholic beverages. (53) This type of drinker was thought to be relatively rare in the United States and Great Britain, but much more common in wine-producing countries such as France and Italy. Drinking for the taste of the alcohol was advanced as an explanation for the drinking problems of many children in these countries, since it was likely that they had learned to like wine and received it as often as they received water or milk.

Chapter Four

ALCOHOLISM TREATMENTS in the 1890s

By 1900 treatments for alcoholism ranged from carefully planned and directed programs at institutions like Ellikon in Germany and Binghamton in the United States to quack cures that claimed to end both morphine and alcohol addiction. Most of these treatments had several features in common. The most important was total abstinence from all alcohol. Discovering the cause of the disease was considered important, and was usually followed by treatment using medical and institutional methods. The major goal of most cures was to restore enough physical and mental health to the inebriate so that he would be able, after treatment, to abstain from alcohol for the rest of his life.

At this point, the various treatments for alcoholism can be divided into ten groups: penal and punitive treatments; institutionalization separate from legal systems; mental treatments, including psychotherapy and hypnosis; temperance societies; drug cures; immunological and serum treatments; health and nutrition cures; radical treatments; quack cures; and religious conversion cures.

When analyzing the different "cures" employed in the treatment of alcoholics, it is well to be aware of several points. First, the estimated numbers of those treated and cured are likely to be quite unreliable. Various persons set different standards for a cure. In addition, spontaneous remission can occur in alcoholics. [50] Finally, people have a tendency to ascribe their cure to the last method tried. [22] General editorial opinion of this time was quick to criticize both the various ways of treating alcoholics and some of the false reporting of cures. [55; 56; 57]

Penal and Punitive Treatments

Legal methods of controlling and treating alcoholism are perhaps the oldest methods for combatting the disease. In general, most of the laws proposed during the 1800s were for the treatment of the occasional drunkard, and were used to incarcerate the drunkard for a short period of time, usually just long enough for the drinker to become sober. He was then fined and released.

The use of legal controls varied from country to country. In the United States, there was great variation from state to state; only some of the states at this time had already passed prohibition.

In Great Britain, the penal system under the direction of J.J. Pitcairn made rapid strides in dealing with alcoholism. Pitcairn [59] criticized the English legal system for treating alcoholics as criminals rather than as sick people; for a person to receive any treatment for alcoholism it seemed that he had either to be quite wealthy or to commit a crime. Unfortunately, prison treatment of alcoholics was generally ineffective, especially with women of the lower classes. Most of these women did not have much in the way of education, training, clean clothes, or food outside of prison, and, as a consequence, Pitcairn [58] reported that the number of women who returned to prison within three months of release was extremely high, with the majority spending ten months out of each year in prison. He further stated that forced abstinence of this kind did not seem to do any good unless it was for at least three years.

France acted much the same as England did in dealing with alcoholics through the legal system. At that time, no institutions existed that were intended exclusively for alcoholics; the only choice for an alcoholic was prison unless he was certifiably insane.[60] Concerned citizens saw the need for changes in the legal system for alcoholic treatment. Some, like Forgue [61], felt the laws should make temperance obligatory. Forgue wrote that for the good of the drunkard, as well as for the good of society, the freedom to get drunk should be restricted. The laws should provide for the internment of any person deemed unable to control his drinking, including those who had not yet had the chance to commit a crime; in addition there should be provisions for self-committal to institutions so that a person would no longer have to be certified insane if he desired institutional treatment. [62] Another proposed system for legal control would have given doctors the right to commit to institutions persons they believed to be no longer capable of controlling their drinking. With the family's assent, a doctor could commit a person whose drinking had not yet reached the uncontrollable stage, but who had a strong possibility of becoming an alcoholic. [63] The French government did not, however, make any major changes in its policy toward alcoholics until 1950.

Austria experimented with a system of court appointed "curators." Curators acted as legal guardians for persons unable to manage their own estates, such as children, idiots, the insane, and those who were generally spendthrifts. During the 1890s, alcoholics who were certified incapable of properly handling their money were assigned a curator and were watched closely. This process successfully controlled alcoholism only among those persons who owned sizable estates; paupers still were not eligible for a legal guardian or for state care unless they had committed a crime. [65]

By 1900, Germany had laws that required abstinence of people in certain professions, penal controls for alcoholics who were convicted criminals, and, in some cities, regulations on drinking age. [66] Forel [67] proposed laws allowing the voluntary commitment of alcoholic persons for a defined length of time in special restrictive institutions. He recommended also that abstinence be promoted by the government and forced, if necessary; that saloons and distilleries be outlawed; and that the only permissable alcoholic beverages be small quantities of fermented beverages produced at home.

In Russia, the problem of alcoholism was dealt with entirely by legislation. Alcoholics who committed a crime were treated like any other criminals. To combat alcoholism, restrictions were placed on the amount of alcohol that could be purchased, prices were made uniform across the country, the number of saloons was sharply reduced, and the percentage of alcohol allowed in a beverage was restricted to 3 per cent. [68; 69]

Across the rest of Europe the legal systems dealing with alcoholism varied. In Hungary, Spain, Portugal, Greece, and Denmark, the only legal means of dealing with alcoholics was to treat them as criminals. Holland had one special institution for alcoholics, although it was mostly for the criminal alcoholic. In Switzerland, several agricultural penal colonies were devoted to the criminal alcoholic. Sweden was on the Gothenburg system, which was very similar to the Russian system and depended mainly on legal restrictions in the sale of beverages for the control of alcoholism: it was illegal for alcoholics to buy alcoholic beverages or for a person to supply an alcoholic with liquor. [60]

In the United States, legal controls on alcoholism varied from area to area. Massachusetts had a probation system that was similar to the curator system of Austria. A person suspected of being an alcoholic was investigated by the court; if he was found to be an habitual drinker or an alcoholic, he was put on probation for a time and assigned a guardian. The same system held for anyone who committed a crime under the influence of alcohol. For a first offense, the person was placed on probation. Offenders who took a drink while on probation were subject to immediate arrest and possible imprisonment.

Wilson [33] explained this strict attitude and prescribed harsh treatment for the habitual drunkard. Those who were classified in any of the disease categories, such as the alcoholic insane or epileptic, were exempt from this type of harsh treatment and were instead placed in insane asylums. Wilson's first proposition was that there should be a legally enforced cultural stigma on getting drunk. Secondly, corporal punishment should be instituted in place of fines for public drunks. Thirdly, since habitual drunkenness was held by this point of view to be nothing more than a deliberately held vice, there should be laws preventing a person from being able to buy enough alcohol to get drunk. Wilson also stated that it was just as much the fault of the society and medicine for the present state of abundant alcoholism because of the lack of laws and the previous common use of alcohol as a medicine. However, he still felt that there was no need for the society to wait until the alcoholic did himself or someone else permanent harm before bringing him to his senses.

There also were a few more radical ways proposed for dealing with alcoholics. Read [34], extending his theory of alcoholic etiology, suggested that the number of alcoholics might be helped, or decreased, even more rapidly, if there were strict laws against alcoholics having any children, since that would decrease the chance of alcoholism being passed among any more generations in the gene pool. He also felt that fewer cases of alcoholism would develop because fewer children would be raised in a home run by an alcoholic person. Objection was taken to some of these suggestions by Vine [72] who said that legislating against procreation would just result in a higher level of infanticide, more deaths at the hands of abortionists and more people unable to support themselves. He suggested, instead, that there be compulsory sterilization of all alcoholics with the idea that this would be both a humane way of treating people in contrast with forced celibacy and this sterilization would more rapidly cut down on the amount of inherited alcoholism.

In Connecticut, intoxication to the point of unconsciousness was regarded by the law as a type of insanity, as was a case of "delirium tremens". No contract made by an intoxicated person was considered binding nor was testimony from a person who had been drunk at the time of a crime allowed in a criminal case.

In many other states, the drunkard was considered insane and, could be incarcerated without any rights in an insane asylum. Courts in New York, Kentucky, Maryland, Illinois, Indiana, North Carolina, Pennsylvania, New Jersey, and South Carolina used similar statutes for processing court cases relating to divorce, contracts, wills and deeds.

Once habitual drunkenness had been established by the court, it was considered sufficient evidence of a person's inability to manage his own affairs. By contrast, in criminal cases the alcoholic was responsible for his deeds. Crothers argued that the laws dealing with criminal cases should be made consistent with those dealing with civil cases, to best protect society and the alcoholic. He based this argument on the idea that "the inebriate who is punished for crime always consoles himself with the faith that he is a victim of plots and conditions that should have been otherwise." (22, p. 284)

At this time, the legal system was still highly involved with having to regulate and prescribe treatment for alcoholics. The laws attempted both to prevent alcoholism by restricting the availability of alcohol and to deal with the alcoholic once his illness had progressed to the point of being a disturbing influence in society.

Several states and municipalities had prohibition laws, with the consequent effect that alcoholics moved to areas where they could more easily obtain liquor. As a result the open towns began to adopt a hard-line approach to the treatment of alcoholics. (71)

Changes were proposed in the laws that would require early treatment for persons who had not yet reached the stage of personal irresponsibility and also for those who had not yet become criminals. Crothers wrote of the necessity of legal means to incarcerate and treat alcoholics, especially those in the dipsomaniac classification, who were not fully in control of their behavior. He argued that it was slightly ridiculous to wait until the dipsomaniac had committed a crime before any steps were taken to control his behavior. Instead, the state had a duty to provide special asylums and to have laws allowing alcoholics to be placed in the institutions before they committed a crime. Crothers [22] also explained the need for an exact, legally supported system of classifying inebriates, so that appropriate legal measures could be applied to each class.

Institutional Treatment

Alcoholism treatments varied from institution to institution, as did the reported cure rates. Some differences can be accounted for in the various types of alcoholics that the institutions were set up to serve; the religious affiliation of an institution, if any; and the laws of the area in which the asylum was situated. Institutions in the United States relied mainly on medical treatment for inebriety, those in England stressed rehabilitating the alcoholic through training and work, and those in Germany combined various sorts of treatments with a heavy emphasis on order and temperance societies.

The idea of institutions was not without its opponents. Some felt that the state should not support institutions to treat alcoholics; instead it should be up to private individuals to run and support institutions if they so desired. Many opponents to institutionalization of alcoholics cited the low cure rates obtained as an indication of the ineffectiveness of this type of treatment. Another argument, advanced mostly by members of the clergy, was that alcoholics should be forced to get well, be treated as criminals so as to encourage them to give up their vice.

The pros and cons of institutional treatment for this period were best summarized by Soltau. The benefits gained from institutional treatment included the constant care of a physician familiar with the disease; the services of other specially trained persons; the help to be gained from other fellow sufferers; segregation from other types of diseases, including mental illness; and the opportunity for further investigation into the cause and the cure of alcoholism. Factors against institutionalization included the difficulty in working with a patient once the acute stage of the disease has passed; problems of separate institutions for the different sexes; adverse effects of older patients on new alcoholics; the time and expense involved; and the difficulty of obtaining well-qualified staff. [72] Nevertheless, at this time institutionalization was by far the most successful treatment for alcoholism. The United States, during the 1890s, was characterized by having special institutions to which a person would go, usually for three months to two years, for a cure. Great Britain, had asylums for the long-term treatment of alcoholism, but most of these were private and required that the patient have some money for treatment or relatives who were willing to support him. In Germany, both long-term and short-term facilities were available; placement was dependent on the severity of the disease.

Short-term institutional treatment usually lasted no longer than ten days; long-term treatment concluded with the total rehabilitation of the alcoholic. In general, the method of treatment in the short-term institutions was to get the person sober, over the delirium tremens if he was suffering from them, feed him, bathe him, and lecture to him that he should not go out and get drunk again; this approach closely resembles our current detoxification system in the United States.

In contrast, long-term treatment undertook the complete rehabilitation of the alcoholic for an extended period of time. The institutions, in many cases, were self-supporting through the work of the inmates, and were located in the country when possible so as to be able to produce as much food and be as self-sufficient as possible. The asylums completely controlled inmates' life, prohibiting visitors, mail, and gifts unless specifically allowed by the director.

One of the best known short-term institutions was the Cery Retreat. The treatment, under the direction of DeMartines, normally lasted for about two weeks, after which the alcoholic was either turned over to a permanent institution on the request of relatives or else was simply released. Cery was originally set up as one of the Keeley Institutes (the description of the Keeley gold cures is in the section on quack cures), but by 1899 the institution had devised its own system for short-term cures. The patient was allowed free movement in a padded empty room; alcohol was withdrawn over the course of about a week rather than immediately. Warm baths were given for an hour each day and the patient was made to walk under supervision for several hours a day in the fresh air. To aid sleep, the institution recommended the use of chloral hydrate, given in a glass of wine, throughout the treatment. [73] At the end of two weeks, the patient was talked to, warned of the dangers of returning to drinking, persuaded to sign an abstinence pledge if at all possible, and finally enrolled in the local temperance society for group support.

Another short-term program was St. Belnnorragies' "Home for Alcoolisme" in France. Here prayer was the major treatment, accompanied by total abstinence. Inmates had the chance to seek work outside the facility and live in the asylum for a while after the completion of the treatment [75]; a similar method is used presently in halfway houses in America.

Those who favored long-term asylums often started by formulating a system to classify alcoholics. Institutions could then set up programs for treating each category, or could specialize in treating a single category. The three major figures in designing institutions for long-term commitments were Avait, Forel, and Crothers.

Avait [44, p. 29] divided alcoholics into three classes. For her first class, the simple drinkers, she recommended treatment in an institution set up specially for the curable drinker and the curable mentally ill. The theory behind this was that a simple case of alcoholism would be amenable to the same types of treatments that were applied to most neurotics at this time.

The second class of alcoholics, the habitual drunkards, needed long-term care in facilities specially set up for their treatment. These should be mostly homes for convalescence; abstinence should be required and there should be light work for the patients. Most, she felt, would need to stay from six to twelve months. Preferably, these homes should care for no more than two hundred alcoholics at one time and be located in the country. Each home should form a self-sustaining community, producing its own food and making items for sale, and should be run by a medical director. There should be close medical supervision during the first month, so that all diseases of the alcoholic could be treated. The major advantage was the increased chance for a cure once the alcoholic was removed from all familiar surroundings, drinking friends, and all other temptations.

Avait recommended placing the third class of alcoholic, the incurable, in an insane asylum. There was no use in trying to treat this class, because most were hardened criminals or persons suffering from various alcoholic psychoses, and, in any case, most had suffered so much physical damage from drinking that there was no way for them to understand or be able to help in their treatment. The penal system should take care of those who were actually dangerous, however.

Forel described five classes of incurable alcoholics and suggested a different type of institution for each. The first class was the chronic drinkers with physical damage. Since these people were not thought to be capable of taking care of themselves or refraining from drinking if released from an institution, even for a short time, Forel suggested permanent institutionalization in homes for such as those described by Crothers.

The second class of incurable drinkers was the alcoholic insane, alcoholics who were suffering from actual mental disturbances, not simply the "delirium tremens". As long as the alcoholic insane were kept temperate, they could be better handled in the insane asylum rather than in a home for the alcoholic.

The third class, the drinking epileptics, were to be treated as any other epileptics and hospitalized if necessary. The primary illness in this group was not alcoholism, but epilepsy; drinking was just a symptom and caused, it was thought, by the same mechanism that caused seizures.

The fourth class was the hereditary alcoholics and this group was regarded as congenitally defective and not really accountable for their drinking. They were thought to require permanent care.

The final class of incurable alcoholics was comprised of the delinquents. This class included sexual deviants, criminals, sadists, and psychopaths, who, in addition to their other problems, were also uncontrollable drinkers. This class was the hardest to deal with, according to Forel, and could not be placed either in the homes for alcoholics or in the insane asylums. No matter where they were placed, they had a tendency to cause trouble. (76;47, p. 528)

The effectiveness of Forel's treatment can be estimated from the report of Oberdieck. He told of almost four hundred men who were treated at Ellikon in 1896 and stated that three hundred forty six recovered enough to be considered cured. (77)

Crothers placed major emphasis on the medical treatment of the alcoholic. His system appeared to be effective in treating alcoholics, with a reported abstinence rate of over 50 percent at five years after the completion of treatment. (50, p. 124) Crothers cited four major steps that needed to be observed in order to obtain a cure. The first step was the complete and total withdrawal from alcohol. Abstinence, he felt, must be complete and permanent. No alcohol should be allowed for any reason - medicinal, fashion, or religious purposes. It should be recognized as a dangerous drug and treated as such. The second step was to find and remove the exciting causes of the alcoholism, which could be rooted in physical or emotional problems. The next step was then to restore the physical health of the patient - turkish baths, a well-balanced diet, and a good amount of exercise were all part of the program. For the final step, restoration of mental health, Crothers suggested first removing the patient completely from his normal environment, optimally to an institution where there was complete control of the patient and his behavior, then applying intellectual stimulation and any psychical remedies that might be of use. Crothers felt that it was the responsibility of the state, as well as of the family, to see that treatment was available to all of those who needed it.

Others who also made contributions to institutional methods of treating alcoholism were Chatelain, DeMontyel, Kerr, and Roseburgh. Chatelain made several suggestions for the treatment of alcoholics in institutions. The first and major point that he made was that all persons who were involved in the treatment of alcoholics would have to abstain themselves in order to win the respect of the alcoholics and to set an example for them. Although Forel had made this point earlier in his writings, Chatelain greatly emphasized the idea and practiced abstention without getting involved in the problems of religious and temperance societies. [48, p. 46; 68, p. 609] Another major step was to restore as much of the patient's physical health as possible by forcing him to abstain completely and by making sure he received a good diet, enough sleep, and exercise. Next the patient was enrolled in a complete military like program. Regimentation of all waking time was enforced and industry was encouraged. At no time were the patients allowed either to leave the home or to have visitors without special permission of the director. The idea behind the isolation was that the patient would recover better if removed from all exciting causes of his alcoholism. Technical recommendations made by Chatelain included treatment of the alcoholic person for no less than six months, certification of all patients as *not* insane, complete control of every aspect by the director, and the location of the establishments as far away from the city as possible.

Alcoholics were divided into five classes by Chatelain: the simple and demented alcoholics, the alcoholic chronic insane, the epileptics, the alcoholic delinquents, and the constitutionally psychopathic alcoholics. His system was designed to help only the first class of alcoholics; the other four classes were to receive other types of institutional treatment. The second class, on occasion, could receive treatment with the first, if the patient was not too far advanced with the disease. If members of the second class were beyond the point of being reached by the temperance societies and the homes, they, along with the epileptics were to be committed to insane asylums. The last two categories, the delinquents and the constitutionally psychopathic alcoholics, were to be placed in special prisons where they would be under guard and carefully controlled. Most of these people, it was felt, could never be cured, but they might at least be able to support themselves if forced to. The cost of the institution should be borne by the individual when at all possible; otherwise, Chatelain felt the funding should come from liquor taxes and special anti-alcoholic legislation. (78)

DeMontyel, in contrast, only deals with two classes of alcoholics: the delirious and the nondelirious. The delirious should be treated in special institutions for as long as it takes to get them over the deliriums. The non-deliriants would be interned by the courts if they were found guilty of a crime or habitual drunkenness. If not, they or their families should be able to request internment in a special institution for the treatment of alcoholism for a defined length of time. If funding was available, DeMontyel recommended setting up separate homes for the criminal and the noncriminal inebriate. DeMontyel's major emphasis is, however, placed on a system of laws to control and combat the spread of alcoholism. [63, p. 517; 62, pp. 335]

The majority of Kerr's work was done in Great Britain, where, as a result of his testimony to the House of Lords about needed reforms in the laws pertaining to the treatment of alcoholics, he was responsible for many of the legislative changes that were accomplished during the 1880s and 1890s. [79] He supported many of Crothers' ideas in the treatment of alcoholics and developed variations of the methods which were used in many of the treatment homes in Great Britain. [80] One variation that Kerr suggested was to assign a probation officer to those alcoholics in treatment who, for financial or personal reasons, could not enter a treatment home. These probation officers would be responsible for overseeing the patient in personal as well as in financial affairs. The family of the inebriate should also be enlisted in the treatment of the alcoholic when it was at all feasible. [81]

Dr. Kerr was also concerned with the increase of inebriety among women and recommended the "cottage system" of home and garden at The Farmfield Reformatory for Inebriate Women at Horley, England. [82] At the Dalrymple Home, along with total abstinence, Dr. Kerr and Superintendent Braintwaite stressed finding an occupation for the inebriate. Religious influences should be brought into play and the reformed drinkers should be encouraged to enter upon temperance and Christian works. Dr. Braintwaite indicated the best age for cure was between forty and forty-five years, with individuals under thirty having little chance of success. [82, p. 160; 83]

One group of writers suggested various sorts of permanent institutionalization for the alcoholic. One major proponent of permanent internment was Bargy. [90] He justified this idea on the basis that by the time most alcoholics were drinking seriously enough to be recognized as alcoholics, they had passed the point of being able to successfully abstain on their own volition and were in need of permanent supervision. This state, he contended, was not the direct fault of the alcoholic, but rather was the effect on the brain of years of alcohol use, causing enough damage to the individual so that he no longer was in control of his behavior.

Brower recommended internment for an extended period of time, but held out hope that the alcoholic, if forced to learn an occupation and kept away from alcohol, would be able to regain his self-control and become a functioning member of the community. He did concur that there would probably be many who would need some kind of group supervision for the rest of their lives, but thought this would be impossible to accomplish outside of an institution.

Parke [30, p. 485] recommended setting up a system of permanent and semi-permanent military-style homes for alcoholics. He felt that most, after an extended period of institutional treatment, would be able to work in the community, but would not have the self-restraint for remaining free from the use of alcohol by themselves. He suggested that alcoholics would be able to work, but that their off-hours be spent in the institution, and carefully supervised. He also indicated leniency in sentencing alcoholics guilty of a first offence. He stated that 95 percent of the alcoholics who did receive a jail sentence for their first offense became chronic offenders. Alcoholics who violated a law during a drunken period should be subject to institutionalization for alcoholism rather than to jail. He also indicated that the only time an alcoholic could be successfully cured was during the period of social drinking which preceded the development of true alcoholism.

Treatment for alcoholics was also being started in Austria and was discussed by F. Manning.[32, pp. 221-223] He recommended permanent institutionalization for most alcoholics, especially those in chronic or insane categories of alcohol classification. All in the inebriate homes should have to work a minimum of six hours a day; the first six hours would pay for the alcoholic's care and any additional hours worked would earn money to be available to either his family or himself. Every possible type of restorative influence should be applied to the treatment of the alcoholic, for in a few cases, it would be possible to effect some kind of cure.

The major reformer in Canada during the 1890s was Roseburgh. He recommended setting up a nationwide system of inebriate homes organized along lines suggested by Crothers and Kerr. He too proposed that most homes should be set up as farm colonies, as far from the major cities as economically feasible, where the inmates could produce most of the food needed. All alcoholics, upon entering the home, should agree to become abstainers; and this pledge should be enforced. Temporary jobs could help the alcoholic earn money while he was still in the home. Those who were able to pay for their care should be encouraged to do so; those who were paupers could be supported by the liquor taxes. (84; 85; 86)

Crothers hoped that by establishing an extensive system of treatment centers, each specializing in the treatment of a certain type of alcoholic, the money that would first have to be invested would be more than repaid to society through the rehabilitation of some of the alcoholics, which would increase the number of productive wage-earning citizens and, reduce the crime caused by many alcoholics. In addition, many families of alcoholic men would no longer be on the welfare rolls, since the head of the family would be able to provide support. This system could be tied into the court systems of the various states, to increase the consistency of treatment of alcoholics involved in court cases, and the legal connection would also increase the likelihood that a person who needed treatment for alcoholism would come to the attention of the courts and not have to be certified as insane in order to receive treatment. Under this system, the origins of the disease could be better investigated.

Crothers envisioned treatment facilities would be of three grades. The first of these would be for new cases and those persons not completely controlled by the disease. The inmates would either be self-committals or those committed by the courts for a period of one to two years. The second grade would treat the more chronic cases, with commitments of one to three years. The final grade would be for those who were generally deemed incurable, and the length of commitments would be five or ten years to life.

The latter type of institution would be the most difficult to operate. The patients were to be organized into military-type habits and were to be kept in the best possible physical condition, allowing for the amount of deterioration they had undergone. Crothers recommended that the inmates provide most of the funding to maintain the institution through their labor, but that each was to be paid a small amount for his work, to be held in trust for him. The second grade of institutions were to be run in much the same way, and the inmates were to be instructed in healthy sorts of amusements, as well.

In the first group of institutions, the inmates would be more tractable to treatment and, therefore, more care should be taken to provide all the necessary mental and intellectual stimulation. The discipline should be quite strict and, if possible, the persons should pay for their care and do enough work in the institution to support themselves. These institutions were really no more than a type of quarantine station that would protect society from the damages caused by the spread of the disease; in addition, the inmates might also benefit from care enough to be cured.

Medical treatments were used extensively in institutions organized along the lines suggested by Crothers. If, upon admission, the alcoholic was inebriated, he had to be sobered up, and cured of the "delirium tremens" if necessary. If sober, he would be assigned to a room and health treatments would start at once. The health treatments usually consisted of proper diet, daily walks, many turkish baths, rides and organized living. In addition, daily religious exercises were emphasized in the majority of institutions. Additional measures were adopted when required in individual cases. The goal of this whole system of treatment was to thoroughly disrupt the pattern set up in the drinking and so break up the causative factors. The patient would have a chance to gain control over himself and, therefore, could be cured of alcoholism. [87; 88]

While asylums such as Washingtonian Hall in Boston, existed in the mid-nineteenth century, the 1870s witnessed a proliferation of inebriate asylums: The Inebriate Home at Fort Hamilton, Long Island; Dr. Jewell's Home of Incurables, San Francisco, California; Walnut Hill Asylum, Hartford, Connecticut; The Pinel Hospital, Richmond, Virginia; Appleton Temporary Home, Needham, Massachusetts; Washingtonian Homes, Chicago and Boston; The Highlands, Winchendon, Massachusetts; Sunnyside, Brooklyn, New York; and Parrishes' Private Home for Nervous Invalids, Burlington, New Jersey. [31, p. 504] These asylums, besides attempting to cure the alcoholic, supplied a ready-made population for doctors to study the disease. The majority of doctors writing in the field of alcoholism during 1870 to 1890 were also superintendents of asylums: T.D. Carothers at Walnut Hill; Albert Day at Washingtonian Home, Boston; and Joseph Parris in New Jersey.

Mental Health Treatments and Hypnotism

At this time, psychotherapy and mental readjustment therapy became more popular in treating inebriates. Though the term "psychotherapy" was not in frequent use in the literature on alcoholism until 1911 (92), many ideas that have been accepted in psychological theory were in use by 1897.

Crivelli (94) wrote that psychological treatments could modify the mental state of the alcoholic and make him more resistant to temptations of drinking. He felt that development of mental character was especially important in the dipsomaniacs. Periodic alcoholics could be helped while in a sober state, aiding them to hold out against an approaching attack of drinking. In this way, one might hope to lengthen the sober periods and shorten the drunken periods in a periodic drinker.

According to Davis (95), mental treatment, should be directed toward instructing the patient in all of the bad effects of alcohol until he sees the reason for abstinence and has developed the willpower to remain sober. The physician should understand as much as possible about the mental make-up of the patient to be better able to adapt the treatment program to the individual and so be more likely to effect a cure by developing proper mental characteristics in the patient.

McMichael, in 1897, expressed the idea that a successful cure for alcoholism should include rebuilding the inebriate's character so that he would recover as much as possible from the mental damage he had suffered while using alcohol to excess over an extended period of time. This could be effected by presenting models the alcoholic could pattern himself after, perhaps even housing him with prominent members of the community, especially the doctors, who could train the alcoholic in work and skills, as well as instruction in good moral characteristics. [6]

Psychological variables were also noticed in conjunction with other new treatments of alcoholism. Atwell [97] noted in his criticism of several of the new serum methods of treatment being tried in France and in San Francisco that imagination and expectation on the part of the alcoholics could very possibly be enough to result in a cure, regardless of the actual value of the treatment. He also made the point that expectations were likely to be a large part of the cure effected in some of the quack treatment homes.

Hypnotism rapidly gained popularity as a cure for alcoholism during the 1890s. Though a few claimed that hypnosis, by itself, could cure a person of alcoholism, most held that hypnosis could be a useful aid. Benedict [53, p. 198] recommended hypnosis as an adjunct to the regular treatment of an alcoholic to be carried on in an asylum. Agreement was voiced by Forel [98] who reported that hypnosis, in many cases, proved as a valuable aid in stimulating the willpower of the alcoholic.

Perhaps the strongest advocate of hypnotic treatment was Burrall. He reported the cure of several alcoholics through the following prescribed method. The patient was hypnotized, then given the suggestion that he did not want to drink any longer. This was repeated for several days, then the time period between sessions was gradually lengthened. In most cases the treatment was successful if started during a dry spell rather than during a drinking spell. Additional drugs were sometimes given to help calm the nerves and hydrotherapy had also proven to be of value. [99]

Other references to the use of hypnotism in the treatment of alcoholism include the one-session treatments of Mason. [100] He reported that, at times, he could hypnotize a person and suggest to him that he no longer desired to drink, without the patient knowing beforehand what the purpose of the hypnotic session was. In most cases, however, it took a couple of follow-up sessions to make the use of hypnotism very effective.

Quakenbos [101] described a complete treatment program for the alcoholic based on a variation of some of the major psychological theories of that time. He described a secondary conscience as a part of a person which contained ideas that the individual did not always know about or would agree with. This second conscience, if brought under control by hypnosis, could conceivably prevent the individual from drinking. Hypnosis seemed to work the best when used with periodic drinkers (dipsomaniacs, under Crothers' classification system) at the time when the person felt that a drinking storm was coming on. Quakenbos stated that most of the time, habitual drunkards could not be helped by hypnotism because they really did not want to be cured. The success of the treatment also depended upon the amount of physical damage that the person had sustained, especially to the brain. After two years twenty out of forty patients treated with this method were still sober, thirteen percent had dropped out of sight, and another seven percent had relapsed without a rebound. This cure rate of 50 percent was as good as the rates reported for other treatment methods up to this time.

In contrast to the American Quakenbos, Sinani [102], reported that hypnotism worked as an added stimulant to willpower, but a treatment program could not use hypnosis as the major treatment for alcoholism. In addition, he recommended it only for those who had not yet reached the stage of chronic alcoholism and who still desired to gain control over their drinking. He also was an advocate of public education on the dangers of alcohol consumption and emphasized the degree of mental damage that alcohol could cause.

Rybakow [104], who did much of his work with alcoholics in Russia, claimed that alcoholics were extremely susceptible to hypnosis. He suggested using hypnosis to help the alcoholic reduce his desire to drink. Rybakow also warned that very few cures could be obtained from the use of hypnotism alone, but it could be used to reach the alcoholic and make him realize the gravity of the situation and, therefore, be more amenable to other types of treatment.

J.M. Bramwell, writing in 1900, stated:

> There is a number of persons, both temperate and intemperate, who are refractory to hypnotism, and it is still a moot question whether the inebriate is more or

less susceptible to its influence on account of his alcoholism. Fortunately, we do not have to depend on a priori reasoning to determine whether the alcoholic is more easily hypnotized we have the facts of experience to resort to. Alcoholized persons are generally good subjects for treatment, but I have never succeeded in hypnotizing a person for the first time, in a state of intoxication. It is necessary to wait until the first effect of the stimulant has passed off. [105]

In London, in 1893, Bramwell treated seventy-six cases of dipsomania and chronic alcoholism by means of hypnotic suggestion, and achieved a 37 percent cure rate. Twenty-eight people maintained three years of abstinence and were considered "recovered." Thirty-six individuals were classified "improved"; they led more productive lives after treatment, although some had relapses. Twelve alcoholics, with twenty hypnotic treatments each, were considered "failures," where no benefit was obtained. Bramwell stated that two conditions were necessary for cure: first, a willing subject and second, a subject susceptible to hypnotic suggestion. Two suggestions were especially effective: the suggestion of nausea if any alcohol was drunk and the suggestion that all alcoholic drinks would taste like Wormwood or castor oil. [106]

Dr. Leslie E. Kelley, writing in 1896, criticized the use of hypnotism on the grounds that "hypnotism does not directly work any real change whatever in the pathology of inebriety or in that of any other disease." [107] It is plausible that Kelley was objecting to hypnotism as treatment, because he believed his own drug treatment was the only effective one.

Temperance Societies

The word, temperance, in its initial inception meant the practice of rational Christian self-restraint. Eventually, it came to refer to the moderate use of food and drink, and after the 1840s, the principle and practice of abstinence from alcoholic beverages. Temperance societies were any organization aligned in ideology and program with the general temperance movement. Some major temperance societies included the Washingtonians, Fraternal Temperance (Band of Hope, Cold Water Army, Sons & Daughters of Temperance, good Templars), Women's Christian Temperance Union, Francis Murphy Movement, AntiSaloon League, Lincoln Legion, and the American Society for the Promotion of Temperance. [108]

The temperance societies espoused various tenets: moderate use of alcoholic beverages; abstinence from the use of distilled spirits; encouragement of drinking beer instead of distilled spirits; abstinence from all alcoholic beverages; total abstinence in a program of social welfare; the formation of community temperance societies; the formation of groups to apply political pressure to pass national prohibition; pledge-signing in evangelistic fashion; pledge-signing among children and young people; increasing restrictions on liquor licensing; movements to make the saloon a club, where liquor would be a secondary consideration; local option; state and national prohibition; and government ownership, control and monopoly sale

of alcoholic beverages to eliminate private profits.
(9, p. 196)

One function of the temperance societies (from a medical point of view) was to provide help and support for the alcoholic after he had finished the main part of his treatment in an institution. Since it was not possible to maintain all of the alcoholics in special institutions, the temperance societies were especially helpful to the simple alcoholics. The people who were not ill enough to be placed in an institution or who had not yet reached the total drunkard stage could be helped by joining a group of people who discouraged the consumption of alcohol.

The Washingtonians, formed in the 1840s, required a pledge of total abstinence and attendance at weekly meetings where members would relate their stories of drunkardness and recovery. As a body, they recognized no religion or creed, were politically neutral, and each member was supposed to help alcoholics who were still drinking. [101]

During the 1870s, reform clubs, were exclusively set up for alcoholics; their distinguishing characteristics was their religious spirit, which included dependence upon God and reliance upon prayer. Dr. Reynolds, founder of the Bangor Reform Club, conceived the idea of reform clubs made up exclusively of those who had been drinking men. He believed, that there must exist between two men who had once been intemperate, a sympathy which could not exist between a man who has, and one who has never, drunk to excess. (31, p. 548)

By the 1890s, Carrie Nation was on the road destroying saloons (she called it "hatchetation"). The Populists were gaining political strength, as was the Anti-Saloon League. The temperance society movement was not restricted to the United States, which during the 1890s was seeing a revival of Washingtonian type movements. In France there were the "Etoile Bleue" and "La Prosperite" helping drunkards; in Germany there was the Blue Cross and the Anti-Alcoholic League. In addition to helping the reformed alcoholics find homes and jobs, the anti-alcohol societies were active in educating schoolchildren against the dangers of alcohol, supporting treatment institutions and promoting active recruitment of alcoholics to fill the institutions to increase the number of alcoholics who had been "saved." (66, p. 559; 18, p. 428; 61, p. 374; 68, p. 609) Most temperance homes for inebriates had weekly meetings organized for mutual help and encouragement. (31, p. 548)

Drug Cures

While it is very hard to estimate the extent of drug use in alcoholism treatment during the 1890s, drugs were used in various combinations to prevent the onset of alcoholic attacks in dipsomaniacs, to ease withdrawal symptoms in chronic alcoholics, to build up the resistance of the alcoholic to various diseases, and to create alcohol aversion. A few of the more experimental treatments included nausea-causing drugs, substitution of a different type of addiction, and the use of marijuana. Very few evaluations of the effectiveness of the various remedies were done and those that are available deal mostly with the treatment of the alcoholic during the acute phase.

Stimulants and cathartics were often used to treat acute alcoholics. Strychnine was a favorite stimulant. Patients were normally given from one sixty-fourth to one twentieth gr. three times a day for about a month and then the dosage was decreased to one sixtieth to one fortieth gr. once a day for several more months. (103, p. 700) Strychnine was thought to combat the craving for alcohol by being a stronger stimulant that blocked both the stimulating and depressing effect of alcohol. During withdrawal, it was thought to provide the needed stimulation without inducing another addiction. (37, p. 48) Contra-indications to the use of strychnine included a tendency in the patient toward extreme nervousness and known liver or kidney damage in the patient. (111) In the literature of this time, one finds many testimonials recommending the use of strychnine in the treatment of the alcoholic, however, most of these do not give any clinical support to the effectiveness. (112; 113; 114)

Arsenic was used as a substitute for strychnine for the treatment of patients who had sustained too much physical damage for the safe use of strychnine or for those who were starting to suffer from strychnine poisoning. Arsenic was administered after each meal and until signs of poisoning started to appear. At that point the dosage was gradually decreased, over a period of several months. [102, pp. 700-701; 94, p. 1473]

Tartar enemic, a cathartic was reported to help stop the craving for alcohol, and also acted as a purge. [50, pp. 121-123; 93, pp. 130-133]

Various compounds of bromine frequently were used to purge, quiet and control the patient. Potassium bromide was the most common compound mentioned; it was thought to have a general sedation effect. [115; 116]

One major difficulty experienced in the treatment of the chronic alcoholic was that the patients had a tendency to develop "delirium tremens" when alcohol was abruptly withdrawn from their systems, especially when it was an involuntary abstinence from drinking. As a result, a wide variety of drugs were used to treat the symptoms. The major treatment for delirium was a combination of purges and rest. G.R. Wilson's suggestions included non-stimulating meals, given at short intervals; mild exercise; plenty of fresh air; and, if possible, much sleep. [117] The intake of vitamins was highly encouraged, along with an increase in fluid intake. [118; 119; 120] Injections of various combinations of minerals were also recommended. [121]

Deaths occurred infrequently and mostly in cases where tranquilizing drugs were used. Sleep-producing drugs were also found to be detrimental to the patient, although they provided a more convenient type of treatment for the hospital staff. (120, pp. 60-63)

Drugs for the inducement of nausea in the patient were also used quite frequently. In order to prevent the alcoholic from drinking as soon as he was released from the institution, he would have to be taught to dislike the taste of alcohol. If the taste of a drink induced disgust in the alcoholic, he would no longer have the desire to drink. (122; 123) Most of the treatments involved inducing emesis as soon as the patient took a drink by the addition of different drugs to the drink, or by adding various substances to food in hopes of training the dislike through ingestion of the drug unknown to the alcoholic. (124; 53, p. 198) Amylic alcohol was reported to kill the desire of the alcoholic for alcohol permanently. (125)

Narcotics also were used for sleep, sedation and to control nervousness in the acute phases of alcoholism. Opium was the most common, but morphine was also used; both drugs were very addictive. (88, pp. 358-362)

Some drugs were used to tranquilize the patient and make him more amenable to other types of treatment. One of the most common drugs used for this purpose was "cannis indica" derivative of the hemp plant. Several varieties of marijuana plant were also available. However, the Indian hemp was recommended over the American variety because of its greater strength. The drug was normally swallowed in a potassium bromide solution. (126; 95; 164; 127)

Less commonly used were bromide salts, which lost popularity because of chronic bromide poisoning; and chloral hydrate and paraldehyde, which had an objectionable taste and smell. By 1903, the barbitals had been introduced into the general medical practice.

Immunological and Serum Treatments

The use of serums in the treatment of alcoholism stemmed from the development of vaccinations for other diseases. The original proposition put forth by Sepalier and Dromard held that an antitoxic substance would be developed in the blood of animals submitted to progressively increasing doses of alcoholic toxins. This substance should then be able to be used to treat alcoholics. This theory failed to explain why people who developed alcoholism did not produce their own antibodies or what the basis was for the physiological dependence on alcohol that had already been demonstrated. (128)

The antibody antiethyline was developed in France by Broca-Soucellier, Sepalier and Thibault, was produced by injecting a horse with alcohol until the horse exhibited physical dependence on alcohol. Blood was then drawn from the horse and the antibody separated from the serum. This substance, when injected into alcoholics, was then alleged to effect a change in the alcoholic so that he could no longer tolerate alcohol. Supposedly, antiethyline awakened the instinctive reflexes of the alcoholic which brought out the "natural" habit of abstinence, [97, p. 349] leaving the alcoholic without any desire for alcohol. The treatment was aimed at both confirmed drunkards and dipsomaniacs, [129] and claimed a 60 percent cure rate out of 57 cases. Several doctors criticized the treatment; they attributed the cures to psychological variables rather than the effects of the actual injections. [97, p. 349; 130] Broca-Soucellier, et al, disallowed the psychological factor argument, since the patients were not informed as to what type of injections they were receiving. They also blamed failures on physical defects in the patients.

Independently, in San Francisco, Evelyn [131] also developed an anti-alcohol antibody which he named "equisine". It too was made from horse blood. After a horse had been injected with alcohol for a period of time, it was bled and the anti-alcohol substance was extracted, sterilized and frozen into small plaques on filter paper. The plaques were then moistened and applied to the scarified arm or leg of the alcoholic, once a week for nine weeks. If any other type of medication was used during the nine-week course of treatment, the serum would not work.

Artificial serums were also developed. These were generally a mixture of unspecified chemicals in a saline solution, which were injected into the patient.

Health and Nutritional Cures

Though most health cures were in conjunction with other treatments, such as institutionalization, a few people claimed to have health cures that could in themselves effect a cure. Health cures usually included supervised diets, rest, work, exercise, and baths.

Food cures were usually popular in areas with a lot of fresh fruits and vegetables. In Germany, one of the most popular food cures was the apple cure. The alcoholic would eat large quantities of apples after meals and any time he felt the craving for a drink. Other fruits commonly prescribed were oranges, grapes, dates, figs, lemons, bananas and onions.

Crothers reported that part of the treatment of alcoholism had to involve careful planning of diet, since most alcoholics, by the time they entered institutions, were suffering from malnutrition. [22]

Charles Palmer suggested that:

> Food which contains too large a percentage of carbon makes continued encroachments on the nervous vitality and health. The nitrogenous elements in food are the most to be regarded, as these seem to reconcile themselves better to the mental and physical processes and to build up flesh at the same time. Fat meats, overcooked meats, pork in all forms, veal, excess of butter, cheese, oils, syrups, tea and coffee must be expunged from the bill of fare, as well as preserves, condiments of all kinds, pastry, and puddings. Let there be plenty of broiled beefsteaks, underdone roast beef, vegetables of all sorts, milk, abundance of fruit both raw and stewed, but nothing that comes from the frying pan.

Cocoa prepared homeopathically, with the fatty oil extracted, is the best drink not only to maintain, but to improve, the purity of the blood. (28, pp. 65-66)

George Wilson recommended that because alcoholics have a poor appetite, especially in the morning, every two hours the patient should eat simple, nonstimulating food. (117, p. 103)

Complete rest was often prescribed for alcoholics suffering from pneumonia, tuberculosis or other drastic physical ailments. (94, p. 1473) Most asylums, however, combined rest treatment with physical exercise such as hiking, riding, and gymnastics. (71, pp. 860-866; 93, p. 136; 74, pp. 130-134)

Hard work was recommended by many advocates of self-supporting institutions. Manual labor was a part of the treatment in many of the institutions, for the financial benefits to the institution and the therapeutic benefits to the patient through learning various skills and having a large part of his time filled. (33, pp. 720-726) In Canada, jobs for inmates in the alcoholic institutions were thought to help them recover faster. Through work, the patients would be able to leave the institution sooner, be able to better resist the temptations of alcohol, could save money, and support their families upon leaving the home. (86, pp. 411-415)

Some religious orders used job placement in their treatment of the alcoholic. By finding him a job in the community rather than isolating him from the area in which they would be living, the alcoholic could redeem himself in his own eyes and in the eyes of the community. Also, it would be easier for the alcoholic to remain in the area for support if he already had a job. Several religious orders also assigned alcoholics duties in the church and in the local temperance societies. (75, p. 502)

Many institutions prescribed baths. Baths were recommended by both Kerr and Crothers as an excellent way to calm and soothe the patient without the use of drugs. Turkish baths were considered especially effective, for they were thought to relax the patient while acting to purge his system. (86, p. 411; 93, p. 133) Baths followed by a massage were considered to be most helpful in the case of the periodic alcoholics and dipsomaniacs. If these alcoholics were hospitalized at the beginning of one of their drinking bouts, Turkish baths were thought to calm the patient and quiet the desire for alcohol enough so that he could gain control of himself. (87, p. 1025; 88, p. 363)

Radical Treatments

The two most common radical treatments were electrical treatments and sterilization of the alcoholic. Electrical treatments were suggested by both Crothers and Sparks. In fact, Crothers claimed that electricity was one of the greatest remedial agents available and that the use of electricity was always followed by an increase in strength and nerve power. Both constant and induced currents were used as "nerve tonics", and were believed to stimulate the growth and repair of damaged nerve tissue. Also called "galvanic" and "faradic" currents, the best assumption is that these must have been terms for direct and alternating currents. Both Crothers and Sparks use the terms "constant" and "galvanic" interchangeably; "induced" seems to be equated in several places with "faradic." Dipsomaniacs seemed to respond most favorably to electrical treatment. Sparks [103, p. 701] suggested a patient receive a daily treatment of constant current for several weeks or, as an alternate, a twenty minute treatment of faradic current also for several weeks.

The sterilization of alcoholics was justified on the grounds that irritating physical causes for their alcoholism might possibly be eliminated. Many doctors believed that alcoholism was largely hereditary; sterilization would reduce the number of offspring in each generation who could possibly inherit the tendency toward alcoholism. In addition, it was felt that fewer people would suffer from the effects of having an alcoholic in the family, resulting in a decrease in the numbers of persons on the welfare rolls. [103, p. 700; 134]

There were other radical treatments that found occasional mention in the literature during the 1890s. Several companies produced equipment designed to treat the alcoholic by stimulation of the nerves in some manner. The two most common types were hot air boxes and light boxes. A hot air box worked something like a Turkish bath; the person was exposed for extended periods of time to hot, dry air in a tight cabinet. Light boxes exposed the patient either to strong light or to ultra-violet light with the idea that some of the effects of climate on

Alcoholism Treatments in the 1890s

the inebriate could be utilized. [22] The climatic theory was described in a paper entitled "The Latest Scientific Vindication for Total Abstinence," presented by Dr. Henry I. Bowditch to the 1872 Massachusetts Board of Health Meeting. Dr. Bowditch condensed his theory into the statement of a general law:

> Intemperance prevails the world over, but it is very rare at the equator. The tendency increases according to latitude, becoming more frequent, and more brutal and disastrous in its effects on man and society, as we approach the northern regions. [7, p. 557]

This theory was dismissed by 1900.

Another radical cure for alcoholism was suggested by an English physician. He observed that when an alcoholic patient contracted a disease that caused great personal discomfort, he soon lost interest in drinking. He noted that gonorrhea seemed to be especially incompatible with the desire to drink. He suggested that if alcoholics were to be inoculated with the organism or forced to contract it, they would soon gladly give up drinking, for at least three months. [135]

Quack Cures

Quack cures were divided into the so-called "gold cures" and those which did not use the "miraculous healing powers of gold."

Some non-gold cures were elixirs, such as gray powder found in the ruins of Thebes that was claimed to have great curative powers when mixed in solution with some other ingredients, or a mixture of lime and potash combined with a different "special" ingredient guaranteed to cure alcoholism quickly and painlessly. (136) Some treatments claimed to cure all addictions, including morphine as well as alcohol. (See table 3, pp. 70-71)

Ironically, many quack cures contained a high percentage of alcohol and narcotics. The American Medical Association discovered that Coblentz' Compound Oxygen contained alcohol, morphine and strychnine. (137) Bradner, reported that few things could damage an alcoholic more than the quack cures containing alcohol, for they could serve only to make the unsuspecting person worse rather than better. (138)

Of the gold cures, those used by the Keeley Institutes were by far the best known.

Various analyses were conducted on the contents of the gold cures. One report said that the Keeley cure, which was claimed to be bichloride of gold was in reality 1/64 gr. strychnine, 1/128 gr. atropine, boric acid and water. The tonic meant to accompany the preceding injection contained tincture of cinchona, aloin and ammonium chloride. In other words, there was no gold in the gold cure. (50, pp.123-127) (table 4, p. 72)

Even if there had been, gold was not physiologically assimilable by the patient and, therefore, could not possibly do any good.

Keeley treated patients with strychnine; half of the patients also received gold. When the patients were unaware of what drug they were receiving, the results of treatment were the same. A third group of patients were told what they could expect to feel and experience as a result of the gold treatment, then were injected with colored water. All had remissions of symptoms and claimed that they no longer felt like drinking.

At first, the Keeley treatment was taken in the patient's home, but after several years' experience it was deemed preferable that treatment should be administered at establishments known as "Keeley Institutes". "Institutes" were established in different parts of America and in foreign lands. The Keeley cure was based on the theory that the nerve cells had been damaged by the poison in alcohol and drugs. Because the nerve cells adapted to the presence of the poison, more alcohol or drugs became necessary. A cure was effected by (1) withdrawing the alcohol or narcotic drug, (2) stimulating the elimination of the accumulated poisonous products through the natural channels, and (3) restoring the nerve cells to their original unpoisoned condition, thus removing the craving or necessity for the liquor or drug.

Another part of the Keeley method was used in many legitimate treatments of alcoholism: a changed environment, rest, proper diet, baths, massage, exercise, as well as administration of drugs. (139; 53, pp. 197-198) Many of the Keeley Institutes were later changed to legitimate treatment homes for alcoholism. (73, p. 575) (141) In 1891, an American organization of Keeley "graduates" had a membership of 3,000 in some 300 leagues, and held several national conventions. By 1918, over 400,000 patients were said to have benefited from treatment at one of the Keeley Institutes.

The Keeley Institutes claimed high cure rates (95 percent over twelve years), but there are indications that the treatments were not any where near that successful. (174, p. 127) For example, one "cure" that was quite widely reported in the literature was of a man who, after years as an incurable alcoholic, was cured by the Keeley method. As a result, he announced that he was going to endow a great cure institute in New York. Before he was able to complete his plans, he died rather suddenly of delirium, the result of a drinking spree.

By 1900, many of the quack cures had been exposed and, since the medical profession was taking more interest in treating alcoholism, fewer quack treatments were able to gain a foothold with a better educated public.

Table 3
Empiric and Charlatan Preparations
(Brander, 1897)

	Percent Alcohol
Dr Buckland's Scotch Oats Essence	35.00

(Also 1/4 gr. morphine to the ounce.) A more insidious and dangerous fraud can scarcely be imagined, especially when administered as this is

Alcoholism Treatments in the 1890s

recommended, for the cure of inebriety or the opium habit.

The "Best Tonic"	7.65
Carter's Physical extract	22.00
Hooker's Wigwam Tonic	20.70
Hootland's German Tonic	29.30
Howe's Arabian Tonic "Not a rum Drink"	13.20
Parker's Tonic	41.60

"A purely vegetable extract. Stimulus to the body without intoxicating. Inebriates struggling to reform will find its tonic and sustaining influence on the nervous system a great help to their efforts."

"Schenck's Seaweed Tonic" 19.50

"Distilled from seaweed after the same manner as Jamaica spirits is from sugar cane. It is, therefore, entirely harmless, and free from the injurious properties of corn and whiskey."

"Boker's Stomach Bitters "	42.60
Brown's Iron Bitters	19.70

"Perfectly harmless. Not a substitute for whiskey."

"Burdock Blood Bitters"	17.60
Flint's Quaker Bitters	21.40
Hoofland's German Bitters	25.60

"Entirely vegetable and free from alcoholic stimulant."

Kaufmann's Sulphur Bitters 20.50

"Contains no alcohol." (In fact, it contained no sulphur, either.)

Rush's Bitters	35.00
Dr. Richardson's Concentrated Sherry Wine Bitters	47.50

"Three times daily or when there is sensation of weakness or uneasiness at the stomach."

Warner's Safe Tonic Bitters	35.70
Dr. Williams' Vegetable Jaundice Bitters	18.50

Table 4
Contents of the Kelley Gold Cures
(de Martines, 1900)

I. Solution 1, given eight times a day, 4 gr. dose

Rp. Auro natr. chlor.	0.72
Strychnin. nitr.	0.06
Atropin. sulf.	0.008
Ammon. mur.	0.36
Aloin	0.06
Hydrastin	0.12
Glycerin	30.00
Extr. cinchon comp. fl.	90.00
Extr. coca erythrox	30.00
Aqua dest.	30.00

II. Solution 2, injected when necessary

1 Rp. Strychnin. nitr.	0.50
Aqua dest.	120.00
Kal. hypermang. q.s.	
2 Rp. Auro natr. chlor.	0.15
Aqua dst.	30.00

Religious Conversion As Cure

At a meeting of the New York Academy of Medicine in 1901, the inadequacy of drugs and medicines as a cure for alcoholism was discussed. The doctors and specialists in alcoholism agreed that religious conversion was the most effective of all cures. To quote Williams James, the only cure for "dipsomania" is "religiomania."

An investigation of religious life and conversion was begun by two psychologists, James H. Leuba and Edwin Diller Starbuck, both of Clark University.

However, the subjectiveness of the divine element in conversion remained an unknown quantity and could only be judged by its positive effects on the individual experiencing it.

Three factors appeared to contribute to the reclamation of the alcoholic. First, and most importantly, was a real desire to be cured. (46, p. 283) Most institutions refused to accept a patient unless he stated his desire to reform. Reform was a prominent religious theme, and very appropriate to alcoholism. Starbuck states:

> Doubtless when there has been waywardness, and one has grown habitually sinful, the most efficacious way of rescue is to picture the fate of continuance in sin, to throw the person back on himself, to lead him to see the blackness of sin as contrasted with the beauty of holiness, and make the break unavoidable, sharp, and final. (142)

In times of remorse and sorrow after a debauche, the contrast of the alcoholic's misery with the happiness of others came out vividly, and the thought of an ideal life came before him. This was strengthened by religious talks, the memory of former religious teaching, and the desire for something better. The distance between the ideal and the real was great and there appeared insurmountable barriers between the alcoholic's present misery and the happiness that might be; but the desire for better things grew, sometimes consciously, sometimes not, until there was a sudden forsaking of the lower life and an embracing of the higher. Thus, conversion and the wish to be cured often occurred together.

The second factor in reclaiming the alcoholic was that after conversion, old associations were altered in a way that helped him in his new life. Individuals who were treated and experienced no conversion might remain temperate, if they did not return to old associations. Usually, though, they were unable to resist, and the control they spent so much time acquiring was lost in the first drink. Conversely, cured inebriates who had undergone conversion were better able to cope with these associations. They usually had a new group of friends with whom to spend their spare time, and may have become involved in helping other people in becoming sober. They were no longer occupied with the thought of drink, and tended to stay cured.

The third factor was that the alcoholic's craving for alcohol was destroyed and replaced by an emotional substitute.

F.G. Peabody [143] stated:

> The drink habit is in a very large degree the perversion of one of the most universal of human desires, the thirst of exhilaration, recreation, and joy; and to remove the only available means for satisfying this normal craving without providing adequate means for substitutes, is like blocking the channel where a stream does harm without observing how many new fields the same stream is likely to devastate. (p. 141)

While various other cures of alcoholism were deficient in this regard, religious conversion was not, and was of such a character as to better supply the emotional need than alcohol itself.

William James expressed his views in his book, "The Varieties of Religious Experience":

> The sway of alcohol over mankind is unquestionably due to its power to stimulate the mystical faculties of human nature, usually crushed to earth by the cold facts and dry criticisms of the sober hour. Sobriety diminishes, discriminates, and says no; drunkenness expands, unites, and says yes. [144, p. 377-378]

Sobriety through conversion, could supply, this "yes" function: without it the individual would seek exhilaration in alcohol again.

Two types of conversion were noted: sudden and gradual. Most conversions of alcoholics were of the sudden type. Active alcoholics between "drink storms" were unlikely to be gradually preparing himself for conversion. There was a period of sorrow after a debauche when an alcoholic would entertain the idea of reform, but these good intentions ceased with the resumption of drinking.

Professor Leuba, in his 1896 journal article, "A Study in the Psychology of Religious Phenomena," [145] began by saying that conversion was the desire of the individual to attain moral perfection and inward clarity. Leuba divided the conversion process into seven subdivisions, corresponding to the natural phases of the experience.

1. *Sense of sin.* Sense of sin was the first manifestation of the religious experience and had two origins. For individuals who had been raised in a strict religious environment and whose belief was that a divine Judge had pronounced sentence, it

became a sense of guilt and of condemnation. The other group had escaped theological teachings or outgrown theological teaching; they felt their sinfulness, internally through their physical and moral misery, and their inability to do what they felt to be right and desired to do.

2. *Self-surrender.* Self-surrender was the turning point in conversion: sense of sin could be regarded as the motivation.

> We might expect to find the will striving with increased ardor as its antagonists yield ground. Strangely enough, that which we commonly term "will" seems weakened as deliverance approaches, and, against all expectation, the victory is won when the self-assertiveness of the individual has given place to complete resignation to "the will of God." (145, p. 327)

Self-surrender was an essential condition of the higher religious life and gave to the individual a sense of confidence, trust, love and joy.

Leuba divided self-surrender into two parts: the "way down" or negative, and the "way up." The positive phase was properly called regeneration; it might be also termed atonement. The negative stage might be named diremption. (145, p. 337) People sometimes stopped either on the way down or on the way up and never completed the process of surrender, perhaps due to intellectual rigidity or resistance.

3. *Faith.* When the process of self-surrender was complete, the affective state changed toto caelo. Despair, guilt and the feeling of isolation were exchanged for joy, the sense of forgiveness, confidence and faith. In religious circles, opinion, belief, and

knowledge were regarded as various degrees of conviction grounded in rational cognition, but faith was different because it was connected with the unknown affective state. (145, p. 348) In the conversion experience, however, faith simply meant a firm conviction and trust influenced by feelings.

4. *Justification*. The sudden relief experienced in conversion was usually interpreted as due to the disappearance of the load of sin. It was taken by the individual as the proof of his justification and of his salvation. (145, p. 349) This could be compared to the sense of relaxation that comes after a period of tension. During this phase, most individuals undergoing conversion stated a sense of release, as though a weight had been lifted off their shoulders.

5. *Joy*. The sense of joy manifested during conversion was inverse in intensity to the "blackness" experienced prior to conversion. During sudden conversion, this joy could be of such a violent nature that the individual might be unable to sleep because everything was illuminated. This sense of perfect lucidity gradually subsided and became a constant sense of peace and satisfaction with the world.

6. *Appearance of newness*. A curious phenomenon was frequently met with at this stage of the conversion crisis. An appearance of newness beautified every object, as if the individual's state of internal harmony had been projected outwardly. The sense of newness often continued for a considerable time after the recovery of peace. (145, p. 354)

7. *The role of the will.* The use of the word will in Leuba's article designated a supposed or real self-determined power of choice. When a person let go of his power in trying to change himself by use of his will and became passive during the conversion crisis, he received, he let God take possession of his being, he yielded, he surrendered. (145, p. 369) The above seven-step model of conversion will be referred to again.

Often, conversion resulted from contact with evangelical temperance groups or with rescue missions run by converted alcoholics. In the 1870s, Gospel Temperance was the first to embrace this idea as a cure for alcoholism, although their interpretation of conversion was usually not very successful in a complete cure. The objective of the Gospel Temperance effort, which might with equal propriety be termed a "moral-suasion effort," was to reform inebriates by appealing to their consciences, better instincts, and religious feelings.(146) Methods included prayer, exhortation, song, pledges, and the church.

During the activities of these groups, thousands and tens of thousands of men felt freed in an instant of time from an appetite that had been growing stronger for years, until it held complete mastery over them; and this freedom seemed to come in answer to the prayer of faith. For awhile this power of prayer was regarded as a force that could break down the liquor traffic and rescue people from the curse of appetite. If prayer were persistent enough and faith strong enough, God would come to the rescue, overthrow the enemy, and redeem and save the wretched victims whom "King Alcohol" was holding in such cruel bondage. (31, pp. 617-681)

Alas, the men who claimed to be "saved" in an instant and had the desire to drink removed were usually drunk again in a short while usually because they had been drunk at the time, did not experience the total surrender process outlined by Leuba, or had been swept away by the contagious enthusiasm at these revivals. Starbuck considered this last point a special danger, caused by the emotionalism and excitement of religious revivals. The effect, he felt, was to induce a state of mere feeling that, when it had passed, left no spiritual residue. When reaction set in, the alcoholic rejected not only his first profession, but the whole of religion. (142, p. 165)

T.S. Arthur wrote that inebriates needed to be pointed toward a higher power for help through both spiritual and physical means; to be perfectly powerless to change themselves; to believe God can and will help if the faith was strong enough; and that the "saved" inebriate, after conversion, must adhere to the gospel of daily right living, love his neighbor, and put his conversion into action. (31, pp. 625-629)

The large gospel temperance meetings ended by the 1880s and were replaced by evangelistic temperance, whose major figures were D.L. Moody and William "Billy" Sunday.

Samuel H. Hadley credited Jerry McAuley with establishing the world's first rescue mission -- where the drunkard was more welcome than the sober man, the thief preferred to the honest man, the harlot favored over the beautiful pure woman -- on October 8, 1872, in New York. (147) Jerry McAuley was born in Ireland in 1837, emigrated to America while still a boy, and made his home in New York, where he fell into evil ways of life and became a confirmed thief. At the age of nineteen, he was sentenced to a term of fifteen years and six months in Sing Sing Prison. There he was converted under the preaching of "Awful Gardner," a former noted prize-fighter whom Jerry had known before going to prison. Gardner's story of his former life and of the change that had come upon him arrested Jerry's attention and led him to seek a similar deliverance. He was pardoned in 1864 by the Governor for his evangelical work; whereupon he took up residence in New York and began his work. (141, p. 1619) McAuley advocated public confession ("telling experiences"), conversion, and concern for helping other drunkards. (17, p. 2134) Aided by his wife, Maria, Jerry McAuley worked until his death in 1894 in the reclamation of drunkards.

One Wednesday evening in 1882, Jerry McAuley helped convert a drunkard by the name of Samuel Hopkins Hadley. After Hadley's conversion, he became an active and successful member of McAuley's Water Street Mission. He even lured his drunkard brother, Colonel Henry Harrison Hadley, down to Water Street one night in July 1886 and helped to convert him. (The Colonel went on to run the St. Bartholomew Rescue Mission in New York and helped with the United States Church Army and the Christian Abstainers' Union). [146, p. 1164] From the 1890s until his death in 1906, Samuel Hadley traveled to Winona to participate in the annual Great Bible Conference, as did representatives from missions across the nation. Great theologians, wonderful expositors of God, successful evangelists and preachers of renown spoke at these conferences, but whenever it was known that S.H. Hadley was to speak the people with one accord rushed to hear him. After his death, August 27th was selected as S.H. Hadley Day and it was agreed that there would always be a representative from Water Street to open the conference with Hadley's favorite saying, "Who being dead, yet speaketh." [147, p. 130]

Hadley's son was converted three days after his father's death. Henry Harrison Hadley II became a missionary like his father and traveled throughout the United States doing Christian work. In 1926 he helped open Calvary Mission in New York City with Rev. Samuel Shoemaker. Over the years, many drunkards were converted at this mission. Men began to change and, as "Harry" Hadley used to say, to "stick." On December 7, 1934, Calvary Mission had a drunken first-time visitor, William Griffith Wilson. This visit helped to precipitate Wilson's last debauche and four days later on December 11, 1934, he entered Towns' Hospital which was to become his final detoxification.

Chapter Five

THE "PROHIBITION CURE"

The Anti-Saloon League emerged toward the end of the nineteenth century: it was to be the last and most effective of the prohibition-temperance movements. Their strategy was to make saloons the target of their efforts. A typical quote from the Anti-Saloon League reads:

> The saloon is the storm center of crime; the devil's headquarters on earth; the school- master of a broken decalogue; the defiler of youth; the enemy of the home; the foe of peace; the deceiver of nations; the beast of sensuality; the past master of intrigue; the vagabond of poverty; the social vulture; the rendezvous of demagogues; the enlisting officer of sin; the serpent of Eden; a ponderous second edition of hell, revised, enlarged and illuminated. (150)

Gradually a campaign was organized to promote national prohibition. Several political victories followed, including overriding President Taft's veto against the Webb-Kenyon Bill, which had been designed to prohibit shipment of alcoholic beverages into dry states. In December 1913, four thousand men and women marched on the Capitol in Washington, carrying a resolution asking for a constitutional amendment to prohibit liquor in the United States. Such a resolution was passed by Congress in 1917, and was ratified by the required thirty-six states on January 16, 1919. (151) Prohibition, characterized by a cartoonist of the time as a tall, gaunt, red-nosed, stovepipe-hatted monster, had arrived. The monster begat speakeasies, rum-runners, illicit stills, smugglers, bootleggers, gangsters and racketeers. The Eighteenth Amendment proved difficult to enforce, and was eventually repealed on December 5, 1933. (151; 152; 153)

Prohibition was an ill-fated social experiment of drinking control that illustrated the consequences of viewing alcohol-related problems as moral and religious concerns. The reluctance of health professionals to accept alcoholism as medical cases most likely invited the intervention of social reformers and their constituency. (152, pp. 21-22)

The alcoholism treatments listed in the previous section continued to be utilized, but to a lesser degree. Reclamation of the drunkard was given less emphasis until Prohibition was over. The Journal of Inebriety folded in 1914 and the interest of American scientists in the problems of alcohol waned during Prohibition. In Europe, meanwhile, interest continued, especially in the areas of metabolic and nutritional studies.

Charles B. Towns

"Here is an odd story of an odd man with odd adventures, whose virile personality backed a nationwide campaign in which not one individual in America was without a personal interest." So begins an article in Colliers magazine, November 13, 1913, entitled "The 'White Hope' for Drug Victims." Of all the cure proclaimers during the first part of the

Twentieth Century, the undisputed king, or perhaps emperor, so magnificent were his accomplishments and so influential his lobbying - Charles B. Towns. He worked at such a high level in national and international efforts to control narcotism and alcoholism that he appeared to many to be above mercenary considerations. (155)

Charles B. Towns was born in 1862 on a small farm in central Georgia. During his youth he broke horses and mules and steers that no other person could conquer. But the farm became too easy for Charlie and he took to railroading. He used his spare time to study arithmetic and grammar. Railroading yielded somewhat to his aggressive disposition, but he soon tired of it and turned his attention to life insurance. Towns, with his threatening index finger, with his hypnotic eye and prehensile jaw, could convince a granite gatepost that it stood in immediate need of life insurance. He set a record for selling more life insurance than any other man had ever written south of the Mason-Dixon Line up to that time (1901). Soon after, he went to New York to seek a larger arena for his talents. There he found something that excited him even more - the stock market. (156) From 1901 to 1904 he was a partner in a brokerage firm that eventually failed.

At this point, a mysterious man whispered to him, "I have got a cure for the drug habits, morphine, opium, heroin, codeine, alcohol - any of 'em. We can make a lot of money out of it." (156, p. 17) Towns was skeptical and asked his own doctor for advice. His doctor stated that the "cure" was ridiculous, but this type of challenge interested Towns and he placed ads seeking "drug fiends" who wanted to be cured.

Towns found a patient and took the "Whisperer," the "fiend," and himself to the old Abingdon Square Hotel, along with three small vials of medicine. After a few hours of extreme pain, the "fiend" wanted to leave, but Towns physically restrained him and gave him a strong sedative. A doctor and stomach pump were sent for, as the patient became violently ill. After forty-eight hours, the patient was able to leave. Towns and his accomplice decided the "cure" needed additional refinement, so Towns began reading all the known literature on drug addiction and alcoholism. Unable to find any more patients, he kidnapped a racetrack agent and forced him through the treatment, which was successful. His reputation soon spread through New York's criminal underworld and he treated many addicted gangsters. During this time, he eliminated the distressing features of the original formula.

Towns believed the formula was now ready for more widespread use and he interested Dr. Alexander Lambert, professor of clinical medicine at Cornell University Medical College and a visiting physician to Bellevue Hospital, in his formula. Lambert was one of then-President Theodore Roosevelt's physicians and he began telling various government officials about the "Towns Cure." Eventually, the U.S government sent Towns to

China to try and help the estimated 160 million drug addicts in that country. He impressed the American delegation to the Shanghai Opium Commission by his apparent success when, in 1908, he claimed to have cured about four thousand opium addicts in China by his method. (155, p. 80)

Towns had arrived, and he was heralded as "an everyday American fighter." Between 1910 and 1920, he helped to frame the Boylan Bill and the Harrison Act. At the same time he operated a very lucrative hospital, located on fashionable Central Park West, which catered to New York's social elite. It was no more than a fancy, very expensive detoxification facility; Towns would not admit anyone unless the fee was paid upon admission or a "backer" guaranteed to pay the fee, which was $200 to $350 for a five-day stay.

Towns claimed a cure rate at 75 to 90 percent, based on the reasoning that if you never heard from a patient again, he no longer needed your services. In his words:

> We have never had a negative result in any case, free from disability, or from an incurable painful condition which enforced the continued use of an addictive drug - such as gall stones, cancer, etc. A little less than ten percent returned to us for a second treatment, a reasonable presumption being that ninety percent from whom we have never heard further after they left our care had no need to consult with us a second time. (157)

After 1920, Towns' standing in the medical world fell while his claims became more and more extravagant. The substances he claimed he could help people with included tobacco, coffee, tea, bromides, marijuana, cocaine, and paraldehyde in addition to opiates and alcohol.

The Towns Cure appears to border on quackery, but Charles B. Towns has left his influence in one important area. During the period from 1910 to the 1930s, Towns encouraged directors of big institutions and corporations to help save alcoholics, while still on the job. According to Towns, there was no greater economic waste among corporations than the alcoholic waste. No employer was getting the best results from the alcoholic, whether he was wholly, or even partially, under the influence of alcohol, or was merely experiencing the apparently slight effects of one drink. (158, p. 105) It appears that Towns was one of the precursors of the Employee Assistance Programs (EAP), now being widely used in the 1980s.

The Emmanuel Movement and Peabodyism

The period between 1900 and 1908 in the United States was considered the beginning of the Era of Progressive Reform. The Evangelical Protestant churches, industry, and labor began to take an active part in encouraging temperance, believing, along with the Anti-Saloon League and the National Prohibition Movement, that the saloon was responsible for many of society's ills. These years also saw the beginnings of the Emmanuel movement in Boston, which had a major influence on lay therapists' involvement in treating alcoholism and on the principles of Alcoholics Anonymous. This section will divide the literature pertaining to the development of the Emmanuel Movement and Peabodyism in chronological order.

Religion and Medicine (1908)

The introduction of the book, Religion and Medicine in 1908 states, "The object of this book is to describe in plain terms the work in behalf of nervous sufferers which has been undertaken by Rev. Elwood Worcester, Rev. Samuel McComb and Isador H. Coriat, M.D., the book's authors in Emmanuel Church, Boston." (159) The movement and the individuals involved in it were influenced by the rise of psychiatry in Europe, the doctrines of Christian Science, the anthropologic work of Darwin, and the work of the American psychologist William James.

The application of psychological principles in the fields of religion and health was being explored intensively in Boston. Worcester, McComb, and Coriat established a clinic where **physical medicine**, psychological suggestion, and the resources of religion were integrated, stressing the interrelatedness of body, mind, spirit. Scientific procedures were employed in diagnosis, case records were kept, and medical specialists were employed where indicated. The clinic included, among the patients, a certain number of drunkards, many of whom responded favorably. After the patient received a physical checkup, a course of relaxation and suggestion was initiated, and in many cases hypnosis was also incorporated. The Jacoby Club was organized for men who were recovering from alcoholism, and through total abstinence, group support, mutual help, and spiritual inspiration, many recoveries were achieved. (160)

The Emmanuel Movement stressed the power of the mind over the body, medicine, good habits, and a wholesome, well-regulated life. This group made free use of moral and physical agencies stating:

> We do not believe in overtaxing these valuable aids by expecting the mind to attain results which can be effected more easily through physical instrumentalities. If a bad headache is caused by eye-strain, or a generally enfeebled condition is obviously the result of a digestive disturbance, a pair of glasses or a belt is frequently far more effective than suggestion. Most religious workers in this field have made the mistake of supposing that God can cure in only one way and that the employment of physical means indicates a lack of faith. This is absurd. God cures by many means. (159, pp. 2-3)

The Emmanuel Group confined its practice to the large group of maladies that were known in the early 1900s as functional nervous disorders - neurasthenia, hysteria, psychasthenia, hypochondria, alcoholism, and so on. Disorders of this nature were peculiarly associated with the moral life, according to Worcester: "They spring from moral causes and they produce moral effects." (159, p. 113) Correct diagnosis was therefore very important, so that physical disease was not confused with nervous disorders.

Along with the scientific side of their work, an equal emphasis was placed on Christian characteristics. The return to the Gospels of Christ and the acceptance of His words in a more literal sense were the aims of the Emmanuel Movement, for a return to first-century Christianity would be more helpful to people than the dogmatic ceremonies then found in most churches. This interpretation of Christianity was later employed by the Oxford Group.

The contents of the book, Religion and Medicine gives an overview of the techniques used by the authors in bringing about positive changes in their patients. The subconscious mind is discussed at length, as is the work of William James. The authors agree with James that subconscious powers of the mind really exist. To reach the subconscious mind, the authors employed suggestion, hypnotism, and auto-suggestion. The epidemiological factors influencing functional disorders are also discussed with emphasis on environmental and hereditary factors.

The final section of this book deals with the therapeutic value of prayer. If a cure was to be effected, a man's spiritual life must be considered: "Man must become conscious of his need and dependence on a Higher Power, and bring himself more and more into harmonious relations with this Power, and this desire goes forth in prayer." (159, p. 304) The authors conclude with four steps in the remedy of functional disorders: hypnotic suggestion; re-education, or restoration of reality to the patient; work, physical exercise, and pastimes; and renewal of spiritual instinct and prayer. In summation, the authors state:

> We have taken our stand fairly and squarely on the religion of Christ as that religion is revealed in the New Testament and as it is interpreted by modern scholarship, and we have combined with this the power of genuine science (psychology and physiology). This we consider a good foundation - the best of all foundations. (159, p. 408)

Mind, Religion and Health (1909)

Robert MacDonald, minister of the Washington Avenue Church, in Brooklyn, New York, wrote this book (161) in appreciation of the work of the Emmanuel Movement. Dr. MacDonald believed in the curative power of Christianity and psychology and sought to add to the published information on the subject. The volume is virtually a collection of sermons outlining the remedial principles of the Emmanuel Movement. In the introduction, Dr. MacDonald makes a point of stressing that William James had given the movement his approval. MacDonald also reminds his readers that this new movement, was inspired on its "manward" side by psychology, and on its "Godward" side by first-century Christianity. (161, p. 262) He agreed with the Gospel of James that "Faith without works is dead."

The phases of the "cure" used by the movement were also reviewed in this book. The first phase was "confession," wherein the patient unburdened himself of his worries, confessing his follies and indulgences that went back for years. Dr. Worcester felt sufferers could benefit from the opportunity to free his mind to a sympathetic listener. It also opened avenues for insight into the nature of the person's malady, so that curative suggestion could be applied more easily.

The second phase was the imparting of religious faith. To a person whose personality had been submerged in immorality, unbelief, or the empty realization of the senses and is therefore depressed and inert, comes the message of hope and faith in God. He is proclaimed as a present, nearby strength, ready to put His infinite power into that life if the person would ask His help. Christ is represented as the giver of rest and peace. The afflicted soul receives the hopefulness offered and for the first time is able to rest and sleep in the new assurance that all is well.

The third phase of the remedy was in remoralizing the life. Emotions had a very apparent and violent influence upon the nervous system, the digestive organs, and the action of the heart. If fear and worry filled one's life, physical derangement inevitably resulted. "How necessary then to banish fear, worry, and grief and install in their stead the pleasing, cheerful, and joyous emotions, for we will someday learn, God grant soon, that if love and peace pervade the soul, the entire body responds to these health-restorers and a normal state of our functional life results." (161, pp. 252-253)

The fourth remedial phase was the application of "suggestion." The patient was put into a relaxed, quiet state; the will relaxed its striving, the mind and body sank down into rest. Complete surrender of the individual to the universal life was realized. The depths of the subconscious self were laid bare, and into these depths, where evil habit was rooted, were put suggestions of health and strength and victory. (161, p. 254) This was realized through the use of hypnosis and autosuggestion. MacDonald illustrated various case studies dealing with alcoholism, in which once the patient had been guided through the above four phases, emphasis was placed on individual responsibility and daily prayer to maintain abstinence.

MacDonald attempted in this book to clarify the principles of the Emmanuel Movement, even including a question and answer section at the end of the volume. His prejudices slant the book toward Christianity and spirituality with a minimal outline of actual technique. Not until the following book was published did the treatment of alcoholism get mentioned at length.

Remaking A Man (1919)

The term "lay therapy" literally means treatment by laymen. In the field of alcoholism, it is a term that usually means a particular method of treating alcoholics. (163, p. 139) Before psychiatrists began to consider that alcoholism fell within their province and while doctors as a whole were usually leaving excessive drinkers to the churches, a layman - a "dry drunkard" who had no psychiatric training and no degree, but who had a remarkable insight into the state of the mind of the alcoholic - began to treat alcoholics professionally and to attain measurable results. (164) The man was Courtenay Baylor, who in 1912 began to work with Dr. Elwood Worcester.

Baylor may have been the first recovering alcoholic to present a workable, concise treatment for alcoholics. This opinion is supported by Marty Mann in her book <u>Primer on Alcoholism</u> (12), although popular belief usually places the first professional use of recovering alcoholics in the treatment of alcoholism during the early 1940s in the Yale Plan Clinics at New Haven and Hartford, Connecticut.

Baylor began his work with alcoholics with the assumption that for people who were suffering from an alcoholic neurosis (he ruled out those with definite psychoses or so far degenerated that they were incapable of responding to any method of treatment), the condition to be treated was the same regardless of whether it was the cause or the outcome of drinking. (164, p. 152) He believed that the craving for a drink was the result of a state of mental tension that was akin to physical tension. His first concern was to teach his patients how to relax temporarily; then he would show them how to prevent tension from recurring. To make this state of relaxation permanent an alcoholic must re-outfit his life and acquire a new sense of values.

Baylor writes:

> I recognized that the taking of the tabooed drink was the physical expression of a certain temporary but recurrent mental condition which appeared to be a

The "Prohibition Cure" 95

combination of wrong impulses and a wholly false, though plausible philosophy. Further, I believed that these strange periods were due to a condition of the brain which seemed akin to a physical tension and which set up in the processes a peculiar shifting and distorting and imagining of values; and I have found that with a release of this 'tenseness' a normal coordination does come about, bringing impulses and rational thinking.... Underlying and apparently causing this mental state (fear, depression and irritability), I have always found the brain condition which suggests actual physical tenseness. In this condition a brain never senses things as they really are. As the tenseness develops; new and imaginary values arise and existing values change their relative positions of importance and become illogical and irrational. Ideas at other times unnoticed, or even scorned become, under tenseness, so insistent that they are converted into controlling impulses. False values and false thinking run side by side with the normal philosophy for a time; and then with the increasing tenseness the abnormal attitude gradually replaces the normal in control. This is true whether the particular question be one of drinking or of giving way to some other impulse; the same indecision, changeability, inconsistency, and lack of resistance mark the mental process. In fact, a person will behave like one or the other of two different individuals as he is or is not mentally tense. (162, pp. 6-7; 12-13)

Baylor illustrated this theory: on Monday, the alcoholic may be "normal" and values appear to him in their right proportion. He may honestly feel he will never take nor want another drop of liquor. (By normal, Baylor meant that the alcoholic was coordinating physically, mentally, and psychologically, and was free from fear, depression, exaltation, irritability, or any of the other symptoms of the tense mental condition.) Yet, on Thursday, when he has developed the tenseness that prevents perfect coordination and when, as a consequence, the mental confusion and distorted values have returned, this same man may debate with a sort of second self, finally deciding he needs just one drink. He was fully conscious of both lines of reasoning at first, and he knew perfectly well the chain of events bound to follow "just one drink," yet as the tense condition increased, he yielded to the alcoholic philosophy. He was sufficiently conscious of his real philosophy to debate the question with himself at first, but as the tenseness gradually gained control of his brain, he surrendered to dream values and to the action they justified.

Baylor, when treating alcoholics, never used the word "denial," although he described this characteristic very clearly:

> One important factor not to be overlooked in the alcoholic condition is the absence of any real desire - if not the presence of actual reluctance - on the part of the patient to reach a point of complete normality. It is hard to realize that a person suffering from alcoholism should not want to get entirely well. The patient wishes to have the acute symptoms allayed, but there is an unconscious tendency to secretly hold on to his difficulties while making believe that he is trying to surmount them. (162, pp. 18-19)

Freedom from tenseness, in Baylor's opinion, was a normal mental state in which the entire brain was awake and the man coordinated simply and naturally with his surroundings and within himself.

> I like to describe it by the word "relaxed"; and when I use this term, while I do mean to indicate the opposite of tense, I mean also something far more than a state of mere limpness. Relaxation to me suggests a

combination of suppleness, vitality, strength, and force - a certain intentional elasticity. To induce this relaxed state, the tenseness must first be released temporarily by some means; the patient must then be taught to prevent its recurrence; and in order to make these measures lasting and effective, he must be provided with the inspiration of an entirely new outlook on life - "a new scale of values." (162, pp. 20-21)

According to Baylor, the therapist or "instructor" must first gain the patient's confidence and cooperation by avoiding any possible air of superiority or dogmatic statements. The therapist must also constantly keep in mind the large part that indirect methods play in the successful handling of any patient. Baylor writes, "When he remembers that all personal interviews are one hundred percent 'suggestion,' direct or indirect, and is watchful and skillful he may so arrange his contact with the patient that everything which is said and done - the entire atmosphere - shall contribute to the latter's recovery." (162, p. 27) The terms "suggestion" and "autosuggestion," as used in this book by Baylor, refer simply to the thought of or reaction to something seen, heard, or felt, and to the natural expression of that thought in some physical or mental action.

In reviewing the techniques used by Baylor, similarities can be seen to present-day methods. The use of paradox, double-binding, reframing, and metaphor or story telling were all employed by Baylor during his sessions. By the time a person was recognized and classified as a patient, he was in such a state of mind that he was unable to make a consistent and persistent effort in any one direction.

The fact that the patient was physically and mentally doing nothing about his alcoholism brought him no real rest; he was haunted by a feeling of unhappy guilt because he was not doing what he should. Baylor believed this feeling was an important factor in the patient's general nervousness and disturbed psychic condition and that it must be eliminated before the patient could yield himself fully to treatment. It was Baylor's custom, with condition of this kind, to tell the patient that he must do absolutely nothing for a week or more and to insist upon this, in spite of the patient's declarations that he must be active.

> Inasmuch as he has been accomplishing nothing anyway there is no harm in his continuing his inactivity a little longer; and there is a great mental and moral relief to the patient in the fact that he is told definitely that he must not even try to do anything about his drinking. Now, for the first time since his illness, he is making his body and his mind do what he tells them to do. (162, p. 33)

Baylor believed a patient's attention must be caught in the first session and this attention, developed through interest, curiosity, and desire, would then lead to reconstruction.

> An unexpected manner of approach does much to secure the mental and physical attention at the first session. A person accustomed to harsh treatment and harangue and criticism is unconsciously expecting censure for his drinking from me. To this man I show a quality of personal kindness and attention such as he never thought of; and I explain to him how natural it was that he acquired drinking as the habit to deal with his problems. I try to make him feel an understanding and a sincere sympathy on my part. (162, p. 42)

Baylor would begin the first session more like a host than a therapist, and avoid anything in the nature of a definite diagnosis early in the treatment. Before patient and instructor could work together at all effectively, the patient needed to be relaxed physically and mentally, so the two could work at the same speed. To quiet the patient, Baylor would instruct him to listen to his voice for a two-minute period. He would describe a rapidly moving boat on the ocean that slowly comes to rest in a quiet harbor. With the correct use of voice tone and timing, the patient's racing thoughts were slowed down along with the boat. During the treatment process, Baylor would teach his client how to relax his body, beginning with the head and travelling to the toes, by concentrating on various muscle groups, tightening them separately, then relaxing them.

Although Baylor's technique centered on relaxation exercises, the incorporation of new thoughts was also important. Assigned readings were chosen so that the "man on the street" could understand and benefit from them. Baylor asked the patient to write down, for five minutes at a given hour in each day, his exact thoughts, whether they do of drink or sex or music or murder. This diary was read by Baylor at each session and it enabled him to become familiar with the patient's mental process - with the factors prompting his philosophy. It also brought out many hidden and important thoughts, and helped Baylor learn the patient's mental language, which in turn helped Baylor make himself better understood.

Baylor's hope for a patient was that the mental and physical relaxation techniques would become an involuntary action. Prayer and spirituality were absent in <u>Remaking A Man</u>, and it seems incongruous that a main figure in the Emmanuel Movement would not discuss this aspect in the treatment of alcoholics. Baylor summarized three cases to end the book. These cases were all successful ones because he believed the educational value of failures was almost nil.

The reported recovery rate using Baylor's technique was 66 percent abstinence for one year. It appears that this high success rate was due primarily to Baylor's insistence on the patient being willing and motivated to change prior to being accepted as a client. The following two paragraphs end Baylor's thoughts on recovery:

> An important indication of the patient's recovery, which is revealed in his daily notes and in his conversation as our interviews progress, is the improvement in his thinking process. He comes gradually to distinguish almost unconsciously between true and false thinking, until he learns to recognize any reasoning which does not ring true so promptly that his old "false philosophy" is in evidence less and less frequently.
>
> Gradually he learns his true relation to the forces of life, and so he comes to realize that now he can become in reality whatever he has hoped in the most idealistic moments of his youth. He knows that he is in fact "the captain of his soul," and in a new self-confidence -- in the glorious certainty that he need never fail again -- he finds perfect freedom and happiness. (162, pp. 64-65)

The Common Sense of Drinking (1930)

Courtenay Baylor's method of treating alcoholics was used extensively by others during the 1920s. Naturally he had followers both among the individuals he had restored and among others who were drawn to his work. (164, p. 157) The best-known was Richard R. Peabody. Baylor treated and trained him, and encouraged him to write <u>The Common Sense of Drinking</u>, which Peabody dedicated to Courtenay Baylor. In this book, which became a source book for both alcoholics and therapists, Peabody gave greater form and detailed development to Courtenay Baylor's methods.

Peabody had returned to Boston from military service after World War I seriously disorganized as the result of drinking. Hearing of the Emmanuel Movement, he approached Courtenay Baylor and asked for help. Using the methods outlined above, Baylor was able to help Peabody make a recovery. As often happens, Peabody decided to specialize in the treatment of alcoholism. After a period of academic study in the field of abnormal psychology, he developed a system of re-education, that incorporated modern psychological principles in the treatment of alcoholism. (160, p. 20)

Peabody's treatment program consisted of nine steps:

1. A mental analysis and removal of doubts, fears, and conflicts created in the past;
2. Permanent removal of tension, which was only temporarily released by alcohol, by formal relaxation and suggestion;

3. Influencing the unconscious mind by suggestion "so that it cooperates with the conscious to bring about a consistent intelligent course of action";

4. Control of thoughts and actions;

5. Hygiene;

6. The daily routine of a self-imposed schedule to keep the patient occupied, to train his will power and efficiency, and to give him the feeling that he is doing something about his problem;

7. Warning the patient against unexpected pitfalls;

8. Providing the patient with some means of self-expression;

9. Realization that the same force that drove the patient to disintegration will, under conditions of sobriety, carry him beyond the level of average attainment. (165; 166)

These steps functioned to bring about reactions in the patient that Peabody classified as surrender, relaxation, and catharsis. These three responses from his subjects were the result of his instruction. (166, p. 157)

Peabody began his book with a consideration of what is meant by "alcoholic" as distinguished from a temperate or even hard drinker, and then selected from the former group those who had a right to expect satisfactory results from treatment.

> In that wide latitude between moderation and dipsomania where, for practical working purposes, shall we draw the dividing line which separates dissipation from chronic alcoholism? It seems to me that this somewhat arbitrary distinction should be made at the point where drinking does not cease with the occasion at which it originated, but, on the contrary, is resumed on the following morning and pursued until

drunkenness again results. I draw the dividing line between those to whom a night's sleep habitually represents the end of an alcoholic occasion and those to whom a night's sleep is only an unusually long period of abstention. This type of drinker, once he has tasted alcohol, does not stop until he has been forcibly restrained or until his prolonged excess has temporarily exhausted him. (167)

From the alcoholics as a class, Peabody eliminated certain groups as unfit for treatment. One consisted of people who were psychotic; another was comprised of those who did not sincerely wish to help themselves. A third group, for whom only partial success could be expected, included those who were physically weak or psychopathic. (168)

Of what did Peabody's treatment consist? First, the patient was shown that his problem was thoroughly understood and that he would not be scolded or preached at. These Peabody felt, were amateur approaches to a complex situation. The patient was told that the treatment process required a sustained effort on his part to overcome his habit. Furthermore, if he expected to be shown how to "drink like a gentleman" (167, p. 1200), he should go elsewhere. The alcoholic could never again expect to drink moderately, as alcohol had permanently unsettled his nervous system. Complete surrender to this situation might be difficult, for the misplaced pride that insisted on trying to use alcohol reached far into the unconscious. But, until this surrender was made no constructive rehabilitation was possible.

The patient then received a thorough analysis of his past and present life. The unconscious mind was not explored, but he was told of its existence as a means of explaining certain motivations behind his irrational conduct. (169) His desires and future prospects were discussed at length. Such readjustments to his environment as were feasible were recommended, but the patient was assured that no one ever recovered from alcoholism under ideal conditions, and circumstances that he could not change must be faced courageously. He must learn to adapt himself to his surroundings through an inner poise acquired through knowledge and training rather than by means of an artificial medium. Also, the patient was encouraged to talk freely of his problems as a method of relieving his nervous tension through expression.

Peabody gave two reasons why a patient chose to drink in an alcoholic fashion: first, because he had been fixated in, or had regressed to, a childish state wherein the alcoholic was too naively amused and from which, as an adult, he was too anxious to extricate himself; second, that he wished to relieve a nervous tension that had slowly or rapidly accumulated through his fear of life. This second reason was the real, compelling force that made him drink continuously, against his better judgment. (167, p. 1200) Furthermore, as soon as he recognized that the impulse to drink was a symbolic expression of nervous tension he was almost always in agreement that elimination of tension was the main objective of the treatment. It did not seem necessary to Peabody to uncover the conflicts repressed in the unconscious in order to rid the drunkard of his habit.

To relieve this undesirable state of mind, as well as to put constructive ideas in the unconscious, hypnoidal suggestion was given to the patient after he had been put into a light state of abstraction: total amnesia was not sought or desired. (167, p. 1200) This suggestion strived to be as positive as possible. The patient was told that he would be calmer and more relaxed and that from this calmness and relaxation would come a poise and peace of mind that would enable him to translate his sensible theories into equally sensible and consistent actions. The alcoholic craving was referred to as passing away, and it was suggested that the patient no longer wished to poison his nervous system with something that he had already proved, to his own satisfaction, he could not tolerate well.

On the whole, however, alcohol was mentioned as briefly as possible for fear of the adverse effect of negative suggestion. Peabody gave his patients a preliminary description of the psychological principles involved in this treatment in order that the patient would not have the usual layman's fear of hypnotism. The patient was then directed to practice auto-suggestion before going to sleep at night.

To Peabody, the most essential element in this work was the control and direction of the conscious thought processes. A person literally could think himself out of his habit, for in the long run sheer willpower, no matter how strong, was relatively impotent against misdirected thinking. Daydreaming - past, present, and future - about the "joys" of drinking must be avoided at all cost as it was certain to result in a relapse sooner or later. The alcoholic was not asked to repress the problem, but he must consider it as it actually was, not as it might have been or as he wished it might be now. What his friends could drink was of no importance to him, he was psychologically in a different category and would always remain so. (168, pp. 124-125)

As a means of reintegrating a demoralized person as rapidly as possible, nothing was as helpful as a daily schedule, made out by the patient himself and then rigidly adhered to. But the patient must be absolutely honest with himself and carefully distinguish between legitimate reasons for changing his schedule and rationalizations leading to breaking it. The schedule prevented idleness, made the patient conscious that he was doing something concrete about his condition, and most important of all, developed, through many small acts, an ability to sustain constructive conduct. The judgment of the alcoholic was rarely at fault, but, as he was a specialist at avoiding life, his ability to act on his judgment was often well-nigh atrophied. (167, p. 1201)

Peabody believed in the importance of home reading for his patients, adding that excerpts that appealed to the patient should be copied into a notebook. Books were suggested that would influence the patient in a constructive manner, whether they bore directly on the problem or not.

Guidance through inference could come by reading biographies and autobiographies of men who had become successful. Conversely, literature that dealt with the charms of hedonism, expounding a philosophy of "Eat, drink, and be merry, for tomorrow we die," should be carefully avoided. (170) To Peabody, the two most important books for every patient to read were Arnold Bennett's <u>Human Machine</u> and William James' monograph <u>Habit</u>. (Additional titles suggested by Peabody can be found in appendix A.)

Peabody also wrote out simple ideas pertaining to the elimination of the alcohol habit and the formation of constructive ones. These were written out on some fifty separate sheets, one or two of which were handed to the patient at each visit. Some of these ideas follow:

1. Alcohol for inebriates acts as a mental nerve poison in a manner that it does not for the normal drinker. (170, p. 170)

2. Alcoholism is a disease of immaturity regardless of the actual age of the individual suffering from it. (170, p. 170)

3. If an alcoholic takes a drink he must realize he is doing it solely because he wants to drink and not in response to an external stimulation such as the weather, physical fatigue, or viewing football games are typical "good" excuses. (170, p. 102)

4. The conviction that abstinence for the alcoholic is of supreme importance is an absolute necessity. (170, p. 103)

5. It takes sustained effort to unite the intellectual concept that led the alcoholic to seek help with that consistent form of action that is an expression of an

automatic attitude rather than a monument to willpower. (170, p. 104)

6. The patient must be informed with all the emphasis that can be brought to bear that the sum total of experience to date has shown that if a man has ever been unable to drink in a normal way (in using the word "normal" plenty of leeway is allowed for a good deal of dissipation), he can never drink anything containing alcohol without the ultimate results being disastrous; there is no exception to the rule. (170, p. 96)

7. The minute a man seeks to reform for somebody else, no matter how deeply he may care for the other person, he is headed for failure in the long run. (170, p. 101)

8. A man must make up his mind to do everything in his power to cooperate in such work as there is to be done. Halfway measures are of no avail. (170, p. 99)

9. Suffice it to say, once a drunkard always a drunkard. A fairly exhaustive inquiry has elicited no exception to this rule.

10. The going-on-the-wagon point of view and the giving-it-up-forever point of view have little or no relationship. (170, p. 81)

11. The alcoholic has already found out that he cannot learn to drink normally, and he is convinced that his habit is progressive. (170, p. 49)

12. A man who is on the wagon may be sober physically, but mentally he may be almost as alcohol-minded as if he were drunk. (170, p. 106)

13. If a slip is checked instantly, and a vigorous attitude intervenes, no harm has been done. (170, p. 173)

14. Because of the power of suggestion, a person should not expose himself to very strong and lengthy temptations during the first six months of treatment. (170, p. 175)

15. In addition to negative suggestion and fatigue, overconfidence can also enter into the situation in a

destructive manner. The patient cannot afford to become "cocky" about his temperance. (170, p. 176)

16. Because of their peace of mind, their increased stamina, and new self-confidence, the patients' depression, moodiness, irritability, and anxiety tend to disappear. (170, p. 180)

17. As has been stated before, the alcoholic is more a student than a patient, and he should never be allowed to forget that he is taking a course. (170, p. 161)

18. Appeals to the alcoholic's self-respect or warnings as to future mental and physical disasters seldom do any good. (168, p. 115)

19. Complete surrender is apt to be a difficult thing to accomplish because of the interference of a distorted pride. (168, p. 121)

20. Therefore, all important decisions, i.e., marriage, divorce, job changes, etc., other than the decision to definitely stop drinking, should be postponed until the treatment is well on its way to a successful culmination. (170, p. 130)

The popularity of Peabody's book during the early 1930s cannot be stressed enough. Peabody also dealt with various methods the family of the alcoholic could implement.

Body, Mind, and Spirit (1931)

Twenty-three years had passed since the publication of <u>Religion and Medicine</u> by Worcester, McComb, and Coriat, and although its psychology and science were out of date, it would always have a certain historical importance. While the primary object of <u>Religion and Medicine</u> had been to describe the remedial ministry undertaken at Emmanuel Church, what distinguished the book was its frank recognition of religion and science as the controlling forces of human life and its attempt to bring these two highest creations of man into a relation of helpful cooperation. (171) Body, Mind, and Spirit, by Worcester and McComb, updated and crystallized the ideas of the Emmanuel Movement.

Worcester was a student and friend of Theodor Fechner, Wilhelm Wundt, and William James. Psychoanalysis had advanced since 1908, and Worcester believed in a third transfer, "inward transfer" that could follow negative and positive transfer. When the seat of power and authority was felt to be within the patient, then the physician or teacher was no longer important. This transfer was effected best not merely by a recognition of social obligations, but by religious faith and a spiritual philosophy of life. (171, p. vii)

Body, Mind, and Spirit deals primarily with the works of Freud, Jung, Adler, James, Breuer, Huxley, and McDougall. The topics covered include the subconscious mind, sleep and insomnia, dreams, healing deeds of Jesus and the reality and power of prayer. The above authors and topics are integrated into case studies, which are the primary content of the book.

Worcester thought the Towns-Lambert Treatment was possibly effective with morphine addiction, but he had not found their treatment of value in alcoholic cases. The Towns-Lambert Cure paid no attention to moral or psychical antecedents and conditions. (171, p. 99)

Worcester believed our American society was built on alcohol more than on any other substance or on any religion, patriotic sentiment, or idea. No other cause could be pointed to that had produced so much sorrow and misfortune. Alcoholism, according to Worcester, was one of the four curses of mankind, the other three being cancer, tuberculosis, and syphilis. He believed prohibition was a failure and that had the ten years of that national policy been spent in education, the alcohol problem would have been much nearer solution than it was by 1931. The method of treatment was identical to that of Peabody, with the exception of Worcester's emphasis on a deep faith in Providence and prayer as part of the recovery process.

William James' article "The Energies of Men" so impressed Worcester that with James' permission the Emmanuel Church published and distributed the essay. The leading thoughts of this essay were that people possess a "deeper strata" of power, resourcefulness, and endurance, of which we are not ordinarily aware, but on which we can freely draw in the great emergencies of life. (171, p. 240) There are powers within us of which we are seldom aware, that far transcend those which we habitually use. When an unusual emergency develops, this higher stratum of energy appears to rise higher, to break through the barriers which confined it, so that it freely offers itself to our need, but it takes a real emergency, a great danger, the necessity for super-human effort to call it forth. When it comes to our aid, it appears to us as something "not ourselves," which surprises us.

So men have always been disposed to ascribe their greatest deeds to a higher power and to reject praise. (171, p. 245)

The final section of the book deals with the healing qualities of prayer and the teachings of first-century Christianity.

Two other books belong to the writings of the Emmanuel Movement. Alcohol, One Man's Meat (172), written by Strecker and Chambers in 1938, further clarifies the principles of Baylor and Peabody concerning the treatment of alcoholism. The Glass Crutch (173), by Jim Bishop, is an autobiography dealing with Bishop's recovery under the care of Peabody during the early 1930s.

Peabody as much as anyone probably was responsible for introducing into the popular vocabulary the word "alcoholism" and substituting "alcoholic" for the emotionally charged label "drunkard," (160, p. 20) terms that later spread with the rise of Alcoholics Anonymous. Peabody's program had been criticized on theoretical grounds. (160, pp. 20-21) It was perhaps appropriate for only a limited segment of the alcoholic population, but it provided a stimulus to the treatment of alcoholics that was of major importance.

Chapter Six

THE OXFORD GROUP

While the Oxford Group of the 1920s and 1930s bears little resemblance to Newman's Oxford Movement of the early 1800s, it is striking that both had the same name, both came as an answer to the antireligious reaction following a European war, and both aimed to rekindle living faith in a church gone stale with institutionalism. The first Oxford Movement was, however, distinctly ecclesiastical and looked to the church as its authority. Much freer and unhampered by institutional ties, the Oxford Group was more like a religious revolution. The Group met in exclusive hotels, mingled religion with meals and merriment, and declared itself to be not an "organization" but an "organism." It was a distinctly forward-looking movement.

If you were to ask an Oxford Group follower, "Who is the leader of the Oxford Group?" you might receive the reply, "The Holy Spirit." So confidently did the Group believe in the "guidance of the Holy Spirit" that it had no organized board of officers, but relied on what was called "God control" through men and women who were fully "surrendered" to God's will. Actually, the man who was most often referred to as the leader of the movement was Dr. **Frank** N.D. Buchman.

Frank Buchman was born on June 4, 1878, and reared in a deeply religious Lutheran home of Pennsylvania Dutch stock. He was baptized in infancy and confirmed in the Lutheran Church in Pennsburg, Pennsylvania. As a student at Muhlenberg College and later at the conservative Mount Airy Seminary, he showed no special promise as a religious leader. Accused by classmates of being ambitious, he eagerly took a difficult and poorly salaried parish in Philadelphia after his graduation and completion of a year's study abroad. Within three years he had built up the vigor and life of the church and had established a hospice for young men. Differences arose between him and the official board of the hospice, however, and he resigned his position.

He visited England in 1908 and, while attending the Keswick Convention, dropped in on a little church in Cumberland. A woman was speaking to a very small congregation about "The Power of the Cross."

> Buchman said that this doctrine was one that: I knew as a boy, which my church believed, which I had always been taught and which that day became a great reality for me. I had entered the little church with a divided will, nursing pride, selfishness, ill-will, which prevented me from functioning as a Christian minister should. The woman's simple talk personalized the Cross for me that day, and suddenly I had a poignant vision of the Crucified.
>
> There was infinite suffering on the face of the Master, and I realized for the first time the great abyss separating myself from Him. That was all. But it produced in me a vibrant feeling, as though a strong

current of life had suddenly been poured into me, and afterwards a dazed sense of great spiritual shaking-up. There was no longer the feeling of a divided will, no sense of calculation and argument, of oppression and helplessness; a wave of strong emotion, following the will to surrender, rose up within me from the depths of an estranged spiritual life, and seemed to lift my soul from its anchorage of selfishness, bearing it across that great sundering abyss to the foot of the Cross. (174, p. 306)

Harold Begbie asked Buchman to recall, if he could, the physical sensations of that moment of surrender. He said,

I remember one sensation very distinctly; it was a vibrant feeling up and down the spine, as if a strong current of life had suddenly been poured into me. That followed on my surrender. No; it came at the same time. It was instantaneous. (175, p. 20)

A sense of buoyancy came as the result of this surrender and he went back to the house where he was staying to write letters of apology to the six trustees of the hospice in Philadelphia. The letters read:

When I survey the wonderous Cross
On Which the Prince of Glory died,
My richest gain I count but loss
And pour contempt on all my pride.

My dear friend:
    I have nursed ill-will against you. I am sorry. Forgive me.

Yours Sincerely,
Frank
(174, p. 307)

While he received no reply to the six letters, he experienced a deep satisfaction at having done his part in setting things right. Here was the seed of the Oxford Group principle of restitution. Another principle, sharing, began after his conversion experience in a conversation he had with the son in the house where he was a guest. The boy was very much bored with the Keswick Convention meetings and was considered a "difficult case" by his religious relatives. Buchman found that by simply telling of his recent experience and the ill-will that had stood in his way until the letters were written, the young man responded with interest and within a day was "changed."

Upon recommendation by Dr. John R. Mott, in 1909, Buchman became a YMCA secretary at Pennsylvania State College. Here he spent seven years, trying out, with intense zeal, his plan of direct personal evangelism. The Young Men's Christian Association was founded in America in 1851 with the aim of providing lodgings, assembly rooms, and educational and athletic facilities for young men living away from home. In 1864 the YMCA of North America had passed a resolution endorsing temperance and requesting the various Associations "to make use of such agencies as may seem proper for the accomplishment of this great end." In 1872 "total abstinence" was substituted for "temperance." During the early 1900s, the leaders of the YMCA were also officers in the Anti-Saloon League. [108, p. 2932]

During Buchman's years at Pennsylvania State College, his work and influence seemed to grow. In the spring of 1915, he visited the Orient with evangelist Sherwood Eddy and became acquainted with missionaries and their personal struggles. In 1916 he spent a year as an extension lecturer at Hartford Seminary, a small nonsectarian theological school. He taught various courses including "Principles of Personal Evangelism" and bible study.[176] Back in the Orient in 1917, Buchman became more and more convinced that the principle of personal evangelism was "the essential of all Christianity and the absolute essential of all progress." [174, p. 310] The summer of 1918 saw the first house party (to become a recognized Oxford Group technique) at Kuling, China. Here, Buchman was "guided" not only to write a letter to a railway company admitting certain subtle dishonesties and to make full restitution, but to confess the entire affair at the house party of about a hundred people, some of whom were very prominent. "With the pain of confession," he wrote, "came a complete message that meant victory to many in my audience, composed of people of national influence: members of Parliament, a General, several Bishops, well-known folk from the foreign and Chinese communities." [174, p. 310] He did it with some fear and doubt, but said later that it taught him that "a costly confession may be the price of power. Certain things which concern the public must sometimes be publicly confessed." [174, p. 314]

Another American arrived in Peking during 1917, Samuel M. Shoemaker. He had been sent to China at the suggestion of Sherwood Eddy to help start a branch of the YMCA and to teach as part of the Princeton-in-China program. Not having had much success, Sam was upset and discouraged. In January 1918, he met Frank Buchman, who told him of the four absolutes: honesty, purity, unselfishness and love. (177, p. 24) During this initial conversation with Frank, Sam was at first infuriated over a habitual reply used by Frank: "If you are not having any success here maybe it's that you haven't anything to give them." (178, p. 175) "I saw this was a matter for my will rather than my intellect. I asked myself if I was willing, and then I thought how ridiculous I was ever to think of opposing my pigmy will to the will of God." (178, p. 176) Years later Sam would trace the inception of his ministry back to that night with Buchman, when he decided to let go of self and allow God to guide his life. (178, p. 181)

Contacts led Buchman back to American universities in 1920, where for awhile it looked as if Frank's personal evangelism might result in a religious revival at such places as Princeton, Yale, Harvard, Williams, Smith, and Vassar. Kindred groups also formed at Oxford and other schools in England, and exchange "teams" crossed the Atlantic. By 1924, however, some American universities, notably Princeton, began to oppose Buchman's tactics and the indiscretions that were supposed to occur at Group meetings. Buchman was banned from the campus at Princeton, and followers elsewhere withdrew. Undismayed, Buchman simply entered into a deeper fellowship with those few who remained loyal to him. He later claimed that the problem at Princeton was that most of the criticism of the Group's frankness on sexual matters came from a group of sexual perverts.

Henry Van Dusen, in an <u>Atlantic Monthly</u> article, mentions four qualities as outstanding in Buchman, admitting that the fourth may be the secret of the first three: his uncanny "prevision" of the future; his expert understanding of the inmost problems of personality (Van Dusen observes, "I doubt if there is a psychiatrist in the world whose intuitive sensitiveness to spiritual disease can begin to compare with his in acuteness and accuracy"); his remarkable confidence in his own procedure; and his "absolutely unqualified gift of himself to his God and God's plan for him." Van Dusen's article concludes: "Today [1934] he is the undisputed director of a powerful world-wide enterprise, reverenced almost to worship. But there were years of crying in the wilderness, of criticism and calumny and cutting disdain." [179] This rock-like determination of the leader helps explain the movement, for Buchman required similar determination in his co-workers, and it sustained him during the difficult times of American opposition.

Meanwhile, English clerical followers such as Louden Hamilton, J. Thorton-Duesberry, Howard Rose, and G.F. Allen were slowly being welded into a united team for action. The Rev. Dr. L.W. Grensted, an Oxford professor, was also a supporter of considerable importance in those years. By 1927, quiet meetings and personal contacts at Oxford had enlisted thirty men and women who met for training and preparation at Wallingford, near Oxford. Buchman's intensive team discipline and training now began to produce results. The next two years saw great expansion. Public meetings at the Randolf Hotel in Oxford introduced to increasingly large audiences this group of people who had experienced great benefits in their daily lives by "surrendering" their wills to God. Fifteen Oxford men carried the movement to Holland, and in 1928 Hoard Rose of Oxford led a small team of students on a summer visit to South Africa. Their work in overcoming racial strife led to publicity in South African newspapers, which called them the Oxford Group. Until then, the group had called itself "A First Century Christian Fellowship," but in South Africa the name "Oxford Group" was formally adopted. (176, p. 76) In December 1928, the group got even more publicity when Atlantic Monthly took notice of their growing international importance and printed an article entitled "An Apostle to Youth" by John McCook Roots, describing the work of Buchman. (180)

More and more Oxford students were drawn into this new religious group; when they graduated, they carried its message with them wherever they went. Papers such as the British Weekly and the Canadian Witness began carrying Oxford Group news supplements. In the summer of 1930 the first international house party was held at Oxford. The next summer found seven hundred enthusiasts assembled at three similar, simultaneous house parties. Further team training during the winter of

1931-32 provided more leadership for the rapidly growing movement, and interest and followers increased rapidly. In 1934 the international house party was attended by representatives from forty nations; (181) 10,000 came from more than fifty countries in 1935; (182) and the 1936 meeting at Birmingham found 15,000 people meeting in the largest covered building in England, augmented by 5,000 British visitors over the weekend. The first American National Assembly, in June 1936, at Stockbridge, Massachusetts drew a crowd of almost 10,000. (183, p. 14) In Minnesota alone, there were 40 public and private Oxford Groups, with the most popular house parties in Stillwater. (183, p. 19)

Through it all, Frank Buchman was in touch with an international team that would shuttle back and forth across continents and oceans, sometimes as a whole unit, more often as smaller teams concentrating on special campaigns in large cities. Books and pamphlets poured forth by the dozens. The attention of the secular press was attracted and produced some rather favorable articles. Newsreels of Oxford Group work in Denmark, America, and other countries were filmed by several secular firms.

It is a bit difficult to place the Oxford Group among the religious movements of Christian history. It claimed no historical roots other than the Christian fellowship of the first century. Actually, its resemblance to first-century Christian ecclesiae is rather slight, although both combined strong missionary enthusiasm with a worldwide outreach.

In its protest against formal institutionalism, the Oxford Group resembled the Montanist movement of the second century. (174, p. 30) Its talk of absolute surrender to God and devotion to Christ also seems to echo the Franciscan movement of the thirteenth century, with the exception that the Franciscans went about as "poor men of God," while the Oxford Group teams travelled first class and stayed in the best hotels. The intimate brotherhood of living together in an unorganized fellowship, so characteristic of Oxford Group parties, bears some marks of a similar spirit among the Friends of God of the fourteenth century.

Perhaps the closest historical precedent of the Oxford Group, however, is found in the sweeping enthusiasm of the Methodist movement, begun by the Wesleys in the eighteenth century, especially in the similarity between John Wesley and Frank Buchman. Wesley was born into a strict religious family, followed studies leading to the ministry, and started a slow-growing and persecuted "Holy Club" during his student days at Oxford. He spent several disappointing years in the ministry before experiencing a dynamic conversion at a meeting in Aldersgate Street, London on a spring evening in 1738. (174, p. 283) While Wesley carried on his work with more preaching than did Buchman, and while the Methodists were not as generally welcome in Anglican and other high-church circles as the Oxford Group was, Wesley, like Buchman, was opposed to organizing a new church, choosing rather to organize societies consisting only of "converted persons." This situation was very similar to the Oxford Group "closed meetings." Like Buchman, Wesley traveled a great deal, keeping in contact with his societies and sharing intimately the responsibilities of his work with a few fellow workers.

As Methodism progressed, Wesley organized a financial system, ordained clergy, stewards and superintendents, circuits and annual conferences, and it eventually became a new church denomination, as so many similar movements did. The Oxford Group never took this step.

Except for minor differences, then, and the addition of certain modern touches, the Oxford Group may be classed as a good example of a reform religious movement with a pietistic tinge and an ardent missionary enthusiasm aiming to revive both the church and the world. [185] Such movements have arisen quite regularly in answer to the sterility and stagnation of a church that seems inadequate to stem the tide of immorality and other evils rushing upon it.

Special Techniques of the Oxford Group

When Oxford Group followers were asked about the secret of the group's widespread growth, they often replied, "The only secret is listening to God and following His guidance, regardless of cost or consequence. To that alone the Group owes its phenomenal growth." [185, p. 43] In spite of this naive supernaturalism on the part of its followers, the Oxford Group used certain strategic methods of attack almost universally in spreading the movement. Some of these methods were quite new to religious circles prior to 1930, but most of them have been used widely, in slightly different forms, by all sorts of religious movements and workers since that time.

One outstanding feature of Oxford Group work was that everything was done on the basis of teamwork. All people who had been "changed" or were "surrendered" were considered members of the team as a whole. "Team guidance" usually led to the selection of smaller units to direct house parties, conduct witness meetings, handle publicity, issue publications, manage bookstands, organize parades, or carry out other activities. While members of long experience or of close acquaintance with Dr. Buchman sometimes felt it necessary to exercise authoritative leadership, there was, for the most part, an intense spirit of team loyalty and an insistence that "the Holy Spirit is our only leader." All "guidance" received in team or personal quiet times was "checked with the team" before it was put into action. Team members who felt that something should be done were held to the task of carrying it out, if it "checked." The avowed aim of all this teamwork was to "hold every member up to his maximum effectiveness" in the practices of the Group.

Perhaps the most welded teams were those that traveled. Almost every house party and many of the open meetings featured out-of-town people who had come as a traveling team to relate their experiences in the "Group Way of Life." As a matter of principle, a member of the Oxford Group was not allowed to appear alone anywhere to represent the Group.

House parties were usually held in some fashionable inn, summer resort, hotel, or wealthy home, but they also were held at times in outdoor camps, college dormitories, or other less luxurious quarters. Attendance varied from a handful to two hundred or more. When the attendance was larger, the group was sometimes divided into several simultaneous house parties for increased personal contact. Attendance was practically always secured by invitations, usually printed in the best style and sent by people already active in the Group to their friends or acquaintances. Almost without fail, the invitation mentioned that certain prominent people from far or near would be present. Invitations were also sent to prominent or "key" people in the community. House parties were held for anywhere from a weekend to one or two weeks.

A house party team of Group people usually would meet in advance, often for several days, for training and preparation. This team would remain throughout the house party and not only provided the program, but announced the meetings, planned the presentation of personal witnesses, arranged Bible study, initiated personal informal talks with guests, and otherwise directed the gathering. All this was planned in team "quiet times," usually held early in the morning at six-thirty or seven o'clock before the other guests arose. Most of the team members had an hour's personal "quiet time" before the team "quiet time."

Meetings held for the whole group followed no formal agenda, and were quite unlike the average church meeting. Singing and public prayer were usually absent, although the Lord's Prayer was often recited. Some time was devoted to talks by team members on such subjects as sin, surrender, quiet times, the four absolutes, guidance, and the rationale of intelligent witness. (180, p. 811) In most of the meetings personal experiences were related by a team of a dozen or more people. Separate meetings were held for men and women once or twice during the house party. Much freedom was allowed in scheduling meetings and an emphasis was placed on "no rules" to facilitate the hope for a relaxed atmosphere. Meetings and personal talks were supplemented by a display of Oxford Group books, pamphlets, and newspaper and magazine articles, sometimes referred to by Buchman as "ammunition for the spiritual bombardment of a nation." The informal spirit was aimed to set the whole house party at ease. Psychological barriers fell one after the other within the first day or two of the house party. Mealtimes and leisure hours found little groups of two or three talking about personal religious experiences. While guests seldom acted offended and very few felt that undue pressure was exerted upon them, many began to feel increasingly uncomfortable after a day or two. The only release from this discomfort seemed to be to go through the "surrender experience" suggested by Group workers.

Another method used by the Group to interest people was to invite friends and acquaintances personally or the public generally to an "open" witness meeting at a fashionable hotel. On trips to Akron, Ohio, the meetings were held at the Mayflower Hotel. (Because of the nondenominational character of the Group, these meetings were seldom held in churches.) A previously trained, guided, and checked team of six to sixty people of various walks of life would sit in front, facing the audience. One after the other arose to relate personal experiences. The witnessing teams were usually supported by other Group people in the audience who were trained to make personal contacts, get telephone numbers, and set up luncheon engagements and conferences.

The Oxford Group tried to include celebrities on traveling teams, and at houseparties and meetings. It seemed to be a trait of longstanding with Dr. Buchman that he always wanted to keep company with the great. He was democratic enough and chatted with anyone, but no one could deny that he had an eye for big names. Whether this was a compensation for his frustrations earlier in life or not is hard to determine, but not at all unlikely. If it is correct, one can only say that it was a relatively harmless compensation so long as honesty prevailed in the use of great names in Group publicity. With few and inevitable exceptions, this seemed to be the case. It may also be said that the practice was a master stroke of psychology in appealing to the thousands of frustrated middle-class people whose egos found a welcome outlet in a movement that included the great so-and-so, and the celebrated this-and-that.

To the credit of the Oxford Group, the majority of its international leaders were not overly solicitous toward these great figures, but followed rather a strict personal "soul surgery" in dealing with them in private. Also, the semineurotic hangers-on who were so anxious to be seen with the great, were usually given a cutting, challenging analysis of their motives that either discouraged them or set them on the road to better mental and spiritual health. Among the American personalities associated with the Oxford Group were Mr. and Mrs. Henry Ford, Mr. and Mrs. Harry Guggenheim, Mayor Fiorello La Guardia of New York City, Joe DiMaggio, Rear Admiral Richard E. Byrd, Senator Harry Truman, General Pershing, Mae West, and Mrs. M. Edison Hughes, who was the widow of Thomas A. Edison. (188)

From the very beginning Dr. Buchman filled his speeches with chatty phrases and statements that were passed from lip to lip in Group circles. Some of these aphorisms had come from other leaders, it is true, but most of them were coined during Dr. Buchman's own quiet times. Like any good advertiser, he knew that slogans would catch attention, be more easily remembered, and more readily repeated. (188, p. 160) Some of the slogans that had come to him in his Quiet Times were:

Sin blinds and Sin binds.

Crows are black the world over.

PRAY stands for Powerful Radiograms Always Yours.

When man listens, God speaks.

Come clean.

Constipated Christians.

A spiritual radiophone in every home.

Every man a force, not a field.

Confidence, conviction, confession, conversion, continuance.

Interesting sinners make compelling saints.

World-changing through life-changing.

Such ready-made formulae for personal and social ills were very acceptable to many bewildered people who liked simple answers to problems they faced in themselves and others.

Though the Oxford Group clung to medieval theology in many points, its methods and phraseology were quite modern. Like other active and enthusiastic spiritual movements, it made full use of all available modern methods of reaching people with its message.

In the years following the 1930s, when the Group had reached the height of its popularity, many churches and organizations shifted over to Group methods in their work. House parties, more often called "spiritual retreats" by church circles, are rather common today. Fellowship meetings involving sharing and witnessing have been increasing in practically every church body. Whether the influences have been exerted consciously or not, Oxford Group principles changed the practical aspects of church work today. The Group's influence on the church, spiritual organizations, and self-help group practices in this indirect way was perhaps fully as great as its influence on the personal life of individual members, who themselves helped spread the Group's principles and methods. Bill Wilson was one of these members.

Chapter Seven

WILLIAM GRIFFITH WILSON

Vermont

One of the New England States, Vermont is bounded on the north by the Canadian province of Quebec, on the east by New Hampshire, on the south by Massachusetts, and on the west by New York; it has an area of 9,124 square miles. The capital is Montpelier and its most important cities are Burlington, Rutland and Barrie. The name, Vermont, was originated by the French, "vert mont," meaning "green mountain." The Vermont region was explored and claimed for France by Samuel de Champlain, governor of Quebec, in the course of an expedition against the Iroquois Indians in 1609. The first French settlement was established at Fort Ste. Anne in 1666. The first English settlers moved into the area in 1724 and built Fort Drummer on the present site of Brattleboro. England gained control of the area in 1763 after the French and Indian War. First organized to drive settlers from New York out of Vermont, the Green Mountain Boys, led by Ethan Allen, won fame by capturing Fort Ticonderoga from the British on May 10, 1775, in the early days of the Revolutionary War. During 1776 the representatives of the towns met at Dorset and on January 15, 1777 adopted a declaration of independence and a constitution. Vermont was the first state to abolish slavery and provided for universal male suffrage without property qualifications. In 1791 Vermont became the first state after the original thirteen to join the Union. (108, p. 2750; 192; 193)

Vermont's first settlers were of a religious disposition, many being separatists who had left the established communities on account of religious differences and persecutions. Services were held in schoolhouses and barns before churches were built. Notwithstanding these proclivities toward piety, frequently the first building erected in the settlements was the tavern. These taverns, stationed at intervals along the stage-lines, were the nucleus from which the towns and cities of Vermont grew. (108, p. 2750) Often, town meetings were held in the taverns, which usually also served as the first courthouses. The members of the earliest "Communities of Safety," members of the first legislatures, and early state officers were recruited from the ranks of the tavern keepers.

Thomas Chittenden, the first president of the independent State of New Connecticut and later the first Governor of Vermont, was a tavern keeper and the first executive mansion of the State was Chittenden's tavern. A visitor, describing Chittenden's home, stated that "During the evening the Governor divided his time between the transactions of State business and waiting on his tavern customers at the bar." (108, p. 2752)

The first attempt to restrict the free sale of liquor in Vermont was in February 1772 when the New

York Assembly passed a tavern act requiring licenses for places selling liquor in quantities of less than five gallons. Later restrictive laws enacted by New York failed due to lack of observance in Vermont and it was not until January 24, 1788 that the newly organized government of Vermont framed its first licensing law. Supplementary legislation during the first half of the nineteenth century dealt principally with the licensing system. In 1844 the State passed its first local-option law. This was superseded in 1850 by a short prohibitory act. In 1852 a longer prohibitory law, similar to the Maine Law, was passed. Keller and McCormick define local-option as "the right granted by the legislature of a country or state to the inhabitants of political subdivisions such as counties and towns, to decide whether the trade in alcoholic beverages shall be permitted or prohibited therein or what form it may take." (9, p. 127) In 1880 a lessor's responsibility for a liquor nuisance committed on his premises was established. Laws of 1880 and 1882 authorized search and seizure. A measure of 1886 required scientific temperance instruction in all public schools. Liquor legislation remained in status quo until 1902, when the prohibitory laws were adopted. (108, p. 2752) The laws governing the sale of liquor, passed in Vermont during the 1800s, were the strictest of any state in the Union.

Temperance sentiment began to awaken around 1800 as people believed the State was not successful in restricting the sale of intoxicants to "suitable persons." Organized temperance efforts began with the formation of a State temperance society at Montpelier on October 16, 1828; Vermont being one of the original states to organize such a society. The Women's Christian Temperance Union of Vermont was organized at Montpelier on February 17, 1875. The first women's temperance organization in the State, however, was formed in 1873 at St. Albans and was called the "St. Albans Women's Association for the Promotion of Temperance." In 1855 the Order of Good Templars in Vermont was organized in Pittsford.

Bennington County and Dorset, Vermont

The first township chartered within the State and the first permanent settlement in Vermont on the west side of the mountains was in Bennington County in the town of Bennington, during the spring of 1761. In this County was formed the first organized opposition to the claims of New York to the territory called the New Hampshire grants. In this County the Council of Safety held its meetings previous to the formation of the state government.

On the west line of this County on the 16th of August 1777 was fought the celebrated Bennington Battle, which gave the first check to the proud career of British Army officer, John Burgoyne. The trophies of that battle were, in part, four brass field pieces; two of which were later placed in the capital at Montpelier, there to remain as monuments of the valor of the Green Mountain Boys.

The first Christian church formed within the present limits of Vermont was the Congregational church in the town of Bennington and was organized December 2, 1762. The first settled minister was the Rev. Jedediah Dewey. (192, p. 147) A popular private school was located in the town of Bennington, Union Academy, and was under the patronage of the Baptist denomination. Burr Seminary, at Manchester, owed its existence to the munificence of the late Joseph Burr, Esq. In his will and the distribution of his large estate in 1828, he left $10,000 to found a literary institution in Manchester. The institution was incorporated October 28, 1829 and the school commenced in May 1833. In 1820 an institution was established at Norwich, in this state, under the name of the American Literary Scientific and Military Academy and a commodious building was executed for its accommodation. This institution was under the superintendence of Captain Alden Partridge and continued for several years in a very flourishing condition, having pupils or cadets from nearly all the states of the Union. On the 16th of November, 1834, an act was passed incorporating it by the name of the Norwich University and Partridge became its first president. (192, pp. 124-125)

A considerable proportion of Bennington County is mountainous and broken land, which is only suitable for grazing. But there are, in the valleys and on the slopes, excellent tillage lands from which good crops were obtained. In 1840 there were 104,721 sheep in Bennington County and potatoes, maple sugar, wheat and Indian corn were the largest crop yields. (192, p. 146)

Dorset, Vermont was first settled in 1768 and organized the following year. The Paulet and Battenkill Rivers rise in this town and, with the waters of Otter Creek which pass the northern part, afford some mill privileges which were used for manufacturing purposes. There are two mountains partly in this town, the Dorset and Equinox, which are part of the Green and Taconic Ranges. There is also a cavern in the southern part of some note. There is a good supply of Stockbridge limestone and quarries of marble in this area. The marble is white and highly-sought for cemetery statuary. Dorset has an East Village whose primary industry is in the quarries. (195)

WILLIAM GRIFFITH WILSON (1895-1939)

The Wilson family was among the first inhabitants of Bennington County, Vermont, having immigrated from Scotland to Ireland and then to America. The Griffiths came to America from Wales and settled in Danby, Vermont, around 1768.

In 1865 William C. Wilson married Helen Barrows, one of whose ancestors had built the largest house in East Dorset, a great rambling structure that stood just across from the churchyard. For years this house had been run as an inn called the Old Barrows House, but soon after the wedding William discovered that, along with working in the marble quarries, he enjoyed managing the inn and the name was changed to the Wilson House. (190, p. 17) The story goes that William didn't mind joining his customers in a drink, but a temperance revival meeting converted him to the cause of abstinence.

Helen and the two Wilson sons, George and Gilman, continued to run the inn after William's passing. Gilman, often called Gilly, was fifteen years old when his father died. Gilly attended Albany College in New York State and upon his return asked his lifelong friend, Emily Griffith, to marry him. In September 1894, they were married in a Congregational Church. (190, p. 18)

The Congregational Church, represented by the "National Council," adopted a temperance resolution in 1892. The individual churches were urged that "pastors and churches press the work of temperance education in the Sunday-school and home," commended temperance to "a prominent place in the ministrations of the pulpit," pronounced the results of the liquor traffic to be "so thoroughly evil that . . . the only attitude for Christian people is that of unqualified and unceasing antagonism," and the saloon's power "broods over municipal life like a dark cloud." (197, p. 681) Various well-known temperance workers were Congregationalists, including Lyman Beecher, John B. Gough, Dwight L. Moody and Neal Dow. In 1895 there were approximately 1,500,000 members of the various temperance organizations in the United States advocating abstinence from alcoholic beverages. When the population of 1895 is compared with that of 1980, there would be the equivalent of 5,400,000 members of abstinence societies. (7, pp. 716-719; 198)

The young couple took up residence in a small room behind the bar in the Wilson House. Fourteen months after the marriage, on Tuesday, November 26, 1895, William Griffith Wilson was born. Other than the irony of William G. Wilson being born in a saloon, a review of the literature reveals no predisposition to alcoholism related to dwelling of birth.

The following headlines appeared on the front page issue of the New York Times for November 26, 1895:

> President Cleveland cancels trip to Philadelphia;
>
> Olympia Ballroom in New York opens to music of owner Oscar Hammerstein - Police called to stop rioting of 5,000 who couldn't get in;
>
> Alexander Dumas hospitalized in Paris with abcess on brain; Russia buying armor plate in Bethlehem, Pennsylvania;
>
> Barcelona gunpowder factory explodes killing 80;
>
> Illicit Distillery Captured in New York City - Large Quantities of sour mash found;
>
> No ceremony in church for the marriage of Rockefeller and McCormick today - Bridegroom has attack of Pleurisy - marriage to be performed at his bedside in the Hotel Buckingham;
>
> Statement from St. Paul Minnesota - Secretary of Agriculture Sterling Morton proposes new source of revenue - a proposed tax on tea, coffee, and beer instead of sugar. (199)

In spite of their shared backgrounds, the marriage of Gilman and Emily was not happy; Emily considered Gilly to be a spendthrift, irresponsible, lacking in confidence, and often drunk. (190, pp. 19-21) One night in 1905, after a long and largely silent evening buggy-ride with his puzzled but apprehensive son, Gilman Wilson deserted his family. (191, p.10) Bill gave little evidence of the trauma of his father's departure. His young mother obtained a quiet divorce and resolved to begin again. An exceptionally intelligent woman, previously trained as a schoolteacher, she moved to Boston and began studying for a new career as an osteopathic physician. Bill, age ten, and his younger sister, Dorothy, were left in the care of Emily's parents, Fayette and Ella Griffith. The elder Griffiths proved kindly surrogate parents, yet deep within young Bill ached a feeling of rejection - the more painful because, in his own mind, it was deserved. (191, p. 10) Fifty years later, Bill Wilson, in a speech delivered in St. Louis, reflected on this early period:

> They were wonderful old-fashioned Yankees, a breed nearly extinct today. I was tall and gawky, and I felt pretty bad about it because the smaller kids could push me around in quarrels. I remember being very depressed for a year or more, and then I began to develop a fierce resolve to win. I resolved to be a Number One man. (200, p. 53)

During the next four years, Bill lived in East Dorset and attended the local grammar school. Bill became close to the old couple next door to his grandfather's house, the Landons. Rose Landon would ask Bill to go to the local pharmacy for her medicine. (The medicine was opium powder suspended in beeswax, which she would nibble at during the day.) The empty cobbler's shop owned by Rose's father was stocked with five hundred books and Rose was named the town's librarian. (190, p. 29) Bill Wilson became an avid reader at this time and this love of reading would continue throughout his life.

In respect to Wilson's early education in East Dorset, the influence and teaching of temperance thought was a part of the curriculum. In 1882, under the leadership of Francis Willard, the Women's Christian Temperance Union (WCTU) developed a comprehensive educational program for abstinence and prohibition. By 1900, all states had accepted this legislation. (15, p. 117) The scope of this influence on children has not been reached since.

The Pathfinder series of textbooks on anatomy, physiology, and hygiene were typical of those used in grammar schools around 1910. The text entitled Hygienic Physiology had an endorsement page following the title page that stated:

> We therefore cordially endorse and highly recommend the Pathfinder series for use in schools. Signed Mary H. Hunt, National Superintendent of the Scientific Department of the WCTU. (202)

The following excerpts from this text may have been or were similar to the ideas on alcoholism first introduced to Bill Wilson:

> Alcohol creates a progressive appetite for itself. When liquor is taken, even in the most moderate quantity, it soon becomes necessary and then arises a craving

demand for an increased amount to produce the original effect. Yet this is the universal effect of alcohol. The common experience of mankind teaches us the imminent peril that attends the formation of this progressive poison habit. The most moderate beginning of this habit may lead to the drunkard's grave. (202, p.185)

Worse than this, the alcoholic craving may be transmitted from father to son, and young persons often find themselves cursed with a terrible disease known as alcoholism - a keen, morbid appetite for liquor that demands gratification at any cost - stamped upon their very being through the reckless indulgence of this habit on the part of someone of their Ancestors. The American Medical Association at their meeting in St. Paul, Minnesota (1883) agreed with this statement that the offspring of intemperate parents, "entails diseased and enfeebled constitution upon offspring." (202, p. 185)

So intimate is the relation between body and mind (brain), that an injury to one harms the other. The effect of alcoholized blood is to weaken the will. The one habitually under its influence often shocks us by his readiness to break a promise to reform. The truth is, he has lost, in a measure, his power of self-control. The wretched victim of appetite will now gratify his tyrannical passion for drink at any expense of deceit or crime. (202, pp. 212-213)

Bill Wilson had few, peer friends during these years in East Dorset, but in the early summer of 1908 he met his closest friend, Mark Whalon, a university student ten years his senior. The two passed much time together when Mark was home on vacation, with Bill reveling in his enthusiastic friend's quotations from Shakespeare and Burns, Ingersoll and Marx, Charles Darwin and William Graham Sumner. (191, p. 11)

But ideas were not all that Bill Wilson imbibed during the times he spent with his friend. One dry, but chilly afternoon, returning in Mark's delivery wagon from neighboring Danby, they stopped in a tavern. Bill quaffed hot cider, apparently non-alcoholic, but he also drank in something more - the atmosphere of a rural New England tavern. The atmosphere was not primarily the physical aura of "the warm, friendly smell of wet sawdust, spilled beer, and whiskey," although he could lovingly recall this; rather, it was an emotional and vivid "feeling of being at home, his feeling for the men." In later years, "sometimes he could think of nothing else. He wanted it again." (191, pp. 11-12) On the surface, Wilson had discovered the joy of friendly sociability, of feeling a sense of belonging with others; more profoundly, he discovered the experience of "obsession-compulsion." Here, one begins to see the possible formation of a personality prone to alcoholism. The loss of both parents, few peer friends, self-consciousness of physical size, feelings of rejection, guilt, inferiority, and frequent episodes of depression may have been likely factors.

A decision was reached in the late spring of 1909 to send Bill to Burr and Burton Academy. Grandfather Griffith and Emily were concerned about the future of fourteen-year old Bill. They believed that unless Bill was given the opportunity to be away from East Dorset he might turn out like his father.

The next three years would later be described by Wilson as the time when he was the happiest. He became obsessed with proving his worthiness to his peers. He sang in the glee club, played violin in the school orchestra, and was recognized for his abilities in baseball and football. According to Wilson's 1955 speech:

> In that early period I had to be an athlete because I was not an athlete. I had to be a musician because I could not carry a tune. I had to be the president of my class in boarding school. I had to be first in everything because in my perverse heart I felt myself the least of God's creatures. I could not accept this deep sense of inferiority, and so I did become captain of the baseball team, and I did learn to play the fiddle well enough to lead the highschool orchestra, even though it was a terribly bad band. I was the leader and lead I must - or else. So it went. All or nothing. I must be Number One. (199, p.53)

Bill would listen to his fellow classmates' stories of drinking on weekends and vacation. He knew that booze, especially, could play no part in his scheme. Indeed, at this time it represented an actual enemy because it was so linked with Gilly, and Gilly's departure was something he would not think about. (190, p. 54)

While at Burr and Burton, Bill also became head of the YMCA, at that time a quasi-temperance organization. In addition to providing services for young men, the "Y" stressed that its members be of good moral character and adhere to the organization's code of total abstinence. (108, p. 2932)

Three other important events took place at boarding school. Wilson's disdain for peers from wealthy and socially prominent families became evident, an attitude of major importance in the years to follow. Also, in his drive to become a good baseball pitcher, he injured the socket of his right arm and developed a condition rather like ringbone in a horse. To the end of his life, it prevented his arm from ever being fully extended. (190, p. 52)

The third event can best be related in Wilson's own words:

> I felt secure with grandfather's liberal allowance and the love and respect of my schoolmates. I was somebody, substantial and real, and lacked only one ingredient: romance. Then came the minister's daughter (Bertha), and in spite of my awkward adolescence things were complete. I had romance, security, and applause. I was ecstatically happy.
>
> Then one morning the school principal appeared with a sad face and announced that my girl had died suddenly the night before. I dropped into a depression that lasted for three solid years. I did not graduate from school. I was unable to finish because I could not accept the loss of any part of what I thought belonged to me. The healthy kid would have felt badly, but he would never have sunk so deep or stayed submerged for so long. (199, pp. 53-54)

In the fall of 1914, at the age of nineteen, Bill entered Norwich University, a military college in Northfield, Vermont, considered second only to West Point in the quality of military training. (184, p. 16) Preceding his enrollment at Norwich University, Bill had had heated arguments with his mother over his lingering depression. She had said that most teenagers went through periods of depression and that if Bill would only try he would get over his. Their relationship deteriorated. During the winter of 1914, after breaking his right elbow, he began having mild seizures. These attacks forced him to drop out of school and return to his grandparents in East Dorset. At this time, Bill's grandfather also realized a deterioration in his closeness with Bill.

Eight months after the death of Bertha, Bill had met Lois Burnham while she was vacationing at Emerald Lake near East Dorset. Lois was a receptionist at the YWCA in Brooklyn and four years Bill's senior. Lois and Bill became engaged during the fall of 1915.

When Bill returned to Norwich in February 1916, he was still a freshman. Not long after, Bill was suspended from school as a result of his participation in a hazing situation. In June he was again back at school.

The United States entered the First World War on April 6, 1917. That summer Bill completed his training at Fort Monroe, Virginia, and became a second lieutenant in the Army Artillery. His first assignment was at Fort Rodman, Massachusetts. It was during this time that Bill Wilson took his first drink of alcohol.

One evening he was invited along with some other young officers to a party at the Grinnels in New Bedford. Socialites in the area frequently entertained the troops as their contribution to wartime patriotism. Thirty-eight years later, Bill gave this account of his first drink:

> For the first time in my life I saw a butler. Again came that terrible feeling of inadequacy, that shy inability to speak more than two or three words in a row. It was overwhelming. But that night someone handed me a Bronx cocktail. Liquor had killed off a lot of my relatives and I had been repeatedly warned against it. Still I took this first drink, and then another, and another. Ah, what magic! I had found the elixir of life! Down went that strange barrier that had always stood between me and people around me and I drew near to them. I was part of life at last. I could talk easily, I could communicate. Here was the missing link!

Bill Wilson's first drink, at the age of twenty-two, ended in drunkenness and so began a seventeen-year active drinking career. "From that point on after his first drink, he drank whenever and wherever there was a drink available." (190, p. 102)

Meanwhile, the entry of the United States into World War I was the final impetus needed by the Prohibition forces to see Prohibition become a reality. The Anti-Saloon League, using the hysteria and fear that mounted over the war, began a new campaign, presenting prohibition as "first and foremost a patriotic program to win the war." (15, p. 119)

The marriage of Bill Wilson and Lois Burnham took place in Brooklyn on January 24, 1918. On July 18, 1918, Bill sailed from Boston with the members of the Sixty-sixth C.A.C., with only five months left in the war. He was stationed first outside Winchester, England, and then in France. The war ended on November 11, 1918, with Wilson having seen no ground action. He reported later that his real accomplishment in France was adding brandy, wine, and rum to the list of alcoholic beverages he enjoyed.

Wilson returned from Europe and was discharged from the Army in May, 1919. He and Lois settled in Brooklyn. With no college degree or employable skills, Bill took a series of odd jobs. The transition from rural Vermont to competitive New York City was difficult for Wilson, and appeared to accelerate his drinking. At times he needed to drink in order to be able to think straight and to regain his old clarity. (190, p. 118)

Taking night courses at Brooklyn Law School, Bill envisioned himself becoming a lawyer. It is unclear, however, whether he actually finished law school or not. (190; 184) He may have graduated but there is nothing to suggest that he ever took or passed the bar exam. Instead, he began investigating companies along the East Coast and then selling the information to brokerage firms on Wall Street. Along with a good commission, Bill received stock as part of his salary. His drinking increased during this period, and he stated, "As these fits of depression would descend, I drank liquor more as if it was a medicine." (190, p. 29) Bill became adept at making dandelion wine and bathtub gin, but Lois later reported that he would drink them before they matured and would become violently ill.

Lois had her third ectopic pregnancy during 1923, which led to surgical removal of her ovaries.

The Wilsons never had children of their own and were denied adoption because of Bill's drinking. In her later autobiography, Lois said, "I knew I had done nothing to prevent our having children; yet somehow I could not help feeling guilty. So how could I blame him for the increase in his drinking?" (184, p. 35)

During Christmas of 1923, Bill vowed to stay sober for one year: he was only able to stay with this pledge for two months. It was the first of many attempts to stay sober.

Bill received a physical examination in 1928 from Dr. Leonard Strong, who was married to Bill's sister, Dorothy. Strong confronted Wilson on his drinking. Dr. Strong was able to point out the progressive nature of Bill's kind of drinking (190, p. 148), and listed various symptoms that applied to Bill's frequent arguments and fights in speakeasies, amnesia episodes, arrests for drunkenness, surreptitious drinks and lying. Lois frequently found Bill passed out in the hallway of their apartment building. They separated several times, Lois hoping that Bill would come to his senses and cure himself.

Wilson described that period as one in which "I was drinking to dream great dreams of greater power." (199, p. 55) His drunken dreams were shattered, along with his marginal accounts, when the stock market crashed in October 1929. Suddenly, Lois and Bill were $60,000 in debt. "Without money or sobriety I was discredited everywhere. People knew all too well what I was becoming. Finally I slid down into a state where I was drinking ... to numb the pain, to forget." (199, p.55)

Although financially destroyed, Wilson was determined to display confidence to all those around him. "Tomorrow was another day. As I drank, the old fierce determination to win came back." (202, p.13) Bill obtained a job in Canada, and the Wilsons moved to Montreal in 1930. Financial success returned Bill to his accustomed style. It also brought an increase in his drinking. He drank straight gin, began morning drinking, even started to drink at his office. "But drinking caught up with me again and my generous friend had to let me go. This time we stayed broke." (202, p. 13) His drinking and fights at the country club were the reasons for his dismissal. (190, p.158)

At this time, Lois's mother became ill and she left for New York City. Bill stayed in Montreal but couldn't remember for how long or what he did except for spending a night in jail for fighting. When Bill returned to Lois during Christmas 1930, he was greeted with a look that he would never forget. (190, p. 159): Lois's mother was dead and Bill had missed the funeral. The marriage turned cold and was further affected by the worsening economic depression. Although Bill would occasionally find work (and later be fired), they lived primarily on her income from a job at Macy's.

> Liquor ceased to be a luxury, it became a necessity. Bathtub gin, two bottles a day, and often three, got to be routine. Sometimes a small deal would net a few hundred dollars, and I would pay my bills at the bars and delicatessens. This went on endlessly, and I began

to waken very early in the morning shaking violently. A tumbler full of gin followed by a dozen bottles of beer would be required if I were to eat my breakfast. Nevertheless, I still thought I could control the situation, and there were periods of sobriety which renewed my wife's hopes. (202, p. 14)

December 5, 1933, was the last day of Prohibition in the United States, but it made little difference to Wilson. He had used the word "alcoholic" concerning himself as early as the previous spring. (190, p. 168) He had become bedridden and wrote angry letters to President Roosevelt during this period. He began to think of suicide, considered religion as "pious shit," and experienced repeated head injuries from drunken falls. (190, p. 176)

Two sets of circumstances occurred during 1933 that would have major impacts on his later life. First, during his short periods of sobriety, he renewed his childhood pastime of reading. He studied everything written on the subject of alcohol, including all the self-help books of the period. He even spent hours reading Mary Baker Eddy - much of her Science and Health fascinated him. (190, p. 197) Second, he was admitted to Charles B. Towns Hospital on four separate occasions in 1933 and 1934.

Although Wilson's memory of 1934 was distorted, it was his last year of drinking. He began panhandling, stole from Lois's purse, and pawned their household items to get money for alcohol. His physical health deteriorated; he ate very little or nothing on his two and three-day binges, had days of blacked-out drunkenness, and showed signs of brain damage. He also experienced periods of delirium tremens, secondary impotency, depression, interpersonal isolation, and episodes of being incontinent of bowel and bladder. Dr. Strong had prescribed sedatives so Bill could sleep, and he developed a cross-tolerance of sedatives and alcohol.

On or near his birthday in November 1934, Bill was visited by Ebby Thatcher, a friend from Bill's Burr and Burton school days. Ebby had also developed a problem with alcohol but was now sober. Ebby told Bill that while he had been in jail for drunkenness, he had been visited by three members of the Oxford Group, which Bill had heard about. (190, p. 192) The two men discussed the precepts of the Oxford Group, including confession of one's defects, taking stock of one's self, helping others, admitting you were licked, accepting the fact that booze was more powerful than you, and that a "higher power" would help. (190, p. 194)

Ebby brought along another Oxford member, Shep Cornell, on his next visit with Bill. They talked at length, discussing the serenity of their new lives and their new-found sense of purpose. They touched on the power of prayer and the rewards of meditation. (190, p. 196) Bill disliked Cornell, who reminded him of the rich Burr and Burton boys, but he accepted Ebby's challenge to visit Calvary Church on Twenty-third Street. The church was the Oxford Group's United States headquarters and was led by the Reverend Sam Shoemaker.

It was a long walk from the nearest subway station to Calvary Mission and Bill began stopping in bars as he traveled east on Twenty-third Street. Most of the afternoon slipped by between drinks and he was in a drunken high fettle by the time he finally reached the Mission's front door. Ebby tried to sober Bill up with coffee and a plate of beans before the meeting began. "Tex" Francisco was leading the meeting that day. Upon his return home, Bill gave Lois a full account as to how this experience would help him stay sober. (203)

The following morning, to quiet a slight case of the shakes, Bill began to drink. For three days he never left the house or his bed, and he drank as he never had before. His terror of once again being faced with a sleepless night, tormented by phantoms, snakes, and d.t.'s, left him spent and totally incapable of any rational thought or any action except pouring another drink. (190, p. 202) Finally, Wilson decided that he could think all this out more sharply if he dried out. Acting on the "rational decision," he set off once again to Towns Hospital, drinking four bottles of beer - the extent of Lois' credit at the neighborhood grocery - along the way. (190, p. 19)

December 11, 1934, was a cloudy, cold day with the temperature averaging 20 degrees. Hospital records indicate that Wilson was admitted at 2:30 p.m. There, he underwent the so-called belladonna treatment. Hydrotherapy and mild exercise also helped much at first, (202, p. 16) but he soon fell into a depression. On the second or third evening, Ebby visited and again explained the principles of the Oxford Group to Bill. What followed during that night is best reported in Wilson's own words, spoken twenty years later:

> My depression deepened unbearably and finally it seemed to me as though I were at the very bottom of the pit. I still gagged badly on the notion of a Power greater than myself, but finally, just for the moment, the last vestige of my proud obstinacy was crushed. All at once I found myself crying out, "If there is a God, let Him show Himself! I am ready to do anything, anything!"
>
> Suddenly the room lit up with a great white light. I was caught up into an ecstasy which there are no words to describe. It seemed to me, in the mind's eye, that I was on a mountain and that a wind not of air but of spirit was blowing. And then it burst upon me that I was a free man. Slowly the ecstasy subsided. I lay on the bed, but now for a time I was in another world, a new world of consciousness. All about me and through me there was a wonderful feeling of Presence and I thought to myself, "So this is the God of the preachers!" A great peace stole over me and I thought, "No matter how wrong things seem to be, they are still all right. Things are all right with God and His world." (199, p. 63)

Bill would refer to this event through the years to come as his "Hot Flash."

Frightened by this experience, Bill spoke with the resident physician, William Silkworth. The doctor told him, "No, Bill, you are not crazy. There has been some basic psychological or spiritual event here. I've read about these things in the books. Sometimes spiritual experiences do release people from alcoholism."

The next day more light dawned. Bill could never remember exactly, but was inclined to think that Ebby, visiting again, brought him a copy of William James' The Varieties of Religious Experience, which Wilson devoured from cover to cover. (199, p. 64) It was James's theory that spiritual experiences could have a very definite objective reality and might totally transform a man's life. Some of these experiences, James believed, arrived with a sudden burst of light, while others developed more gradually; some, but by no means all, came through religious channels - there were indeed many varieties. All, however, appeared to have one common denominator and that was their source in pain and utter hopelessness. Complete "deflation at depth" was the one requirement to prepare the recipient and make him ready for a transforming experience.

"Deflation at depth" - these words leaped from the page as Bill read them. For what else was hitting bottom except deflation? Wasn't this what had happened to him when doctors had previously condemned him to insanity or death? Wasn't it the story of every ex-drunk he knew? (190, pp. 213-214)

Wilson also reflected on the story of the man who had helped Ebby find sobriety, a former state senator from Rhode Island named Rowland Hazard:

> Rowland, the man who came to Ebby's rescue, had drunk his way through a fortune and in 1930 had wound up in Zurich, a patient of Carl Jung. For over a year he worked with the great psychoanalyst, then, when all his

hidden springs and the warped motors of his unconscious had been revealed, he believed he had a full understanding of the cause of his obsession and could therefore go on living a sober life. But in a matter of weeks after leaving Zurich, the investment banker was drunk, unacceptably drunk. When he returned to Jung the doctor was frank. There was nothing more that medicine or psychiatry could do for him. There was only one hope: occasionally alcoholics had shown signs of recovery through religious conversion. Jung had no advice about where or how Rowland might prepare himself for this, but he would first have to admit his personal powerlessness to go on living. Then perhaps, if he sought, he might find. (190, p. 214)

This is precisely what Rowland finally did. Upon leaving Jung the second time, he fell into the hands of the Oxford Group. With their evangelical eagerness, they were organized to bring about the exact sort of change Rowland was seeking. After returning to America, Rowland had carried Jung's message to Ebby, who relayed it to Bill.

As Wilson read William James, as he reviewed Rowland's story, and his own story, Bill's mind raced ahead. He began to envision a vast chain reaction that some day would encircle the globe - a chain of alcoholics passing these principles along, one to the other. (190, pp. 214-215)

Bill Wilson was discharged from Towns Hospital the afternoon of December 18, seven days after he had been admitted. Bill then associated himself with the Oxford Group, Sam Shoemaker's Calvary Mission, and Towns Hospital. Later he described his behavior at this time as twin jet propulsion - part genuine spirituality, part the old power drive to be number one. There was a kind of young madness in this new and magnificent obsession of Bill's to try to sober up drunks all alone. (190, p. 215) But after six months, Bill could not honestly say that he had helped one alcoholic to sobriety. Bill asked Dr. Silkworth what he was doing wrong, what had gone so amiss with the "deflation technique"? The old doctor decided to give it to him straight:

> "For God's sake, stop preaching," Silkworth said, "you're scaring the poor drunks half crazy. They want to get sober, but you're telling them they can only do it as you did, by some special hot flash... You've got the cart before the horse, boy. Hit them with the physical first" - he kept saying this - "and hit them hard. Tell about the obsession and the physical sensitivity they are developing that will condemn them to go mad or die. Pour it on. Say it's lethal as cancer." Silkworth believed this approach might "crack" them: then Bill could do his God talk. "A drunk," said Silkworth, "must be led, not pushed." (190, p. 217) Silkworth convinced Bill that alcoholism was an obsession of the mind coupled to increasing physical sensitivity: he called this his "allergy theory."

During these months, the Wilsons had been living on Lois's salary, but the time had come for Bill to start earning some money. A business deal took Bill to Akron, Ohio, in May 1935. The deal ended in failure and Bill tried to find Oxford Group members in Akron, as he was thinking of drinking. He phoned Henrietta Seiberling of the Goodyear Tire family and visited with her. She mentioned a Dr. Robert Smith, an Oxford member and an alcoholic, a person Wilson could possibly help. After working with Wilson for a month, Smith took his last drink on

June 10, 1935, the founding date of Alcoholics Anonymous.

Lois visited Bill and the Smiths in Akron during her vacation. Upon the Wilsons' return to Brooklyn they let many alcoholics stay with them. Their attempts to sober up these boarders were not very successful. "We thought we could feed our charges at low cost and pick up a lot of knowledge about alcoholism. As it turned out, we did not sober up a single one. But we did pick up a lot of knowledge." (199, p. 73) On November 18, 1936, Ebby came to live at the Wilsons, but the following May Ebby got drunk; he would have many other relapses and institutionalizations, continuing into the 1950s. (184, p. 197; 191, p. 252)

During 1936, Bill Wilson divided his time between Sam Shoemaker's Oxford Group, Calvary Mission, and Towns Hospital. A small nucleus of sober alcoholics began meeting weekly at the Wilsons' home and some were showing signs of real recovery. The members of the yet-unnamed group also attended Oxford Group meetings and utilized those techniques and principles to remain sober.

In December 1936, Wilson met with Charlie Towns and his associate, Alexander Lambert, M.D. Bill knew all about the lucrative enterprise Towns had been involved in in the boom days of the twenties when wealthy actors and famous playboys had been willing to pour thousands of dollars a week into Towns' till for a little discreet drying out. What Bill didn't know was how gravely the business had been dropping off in recent years, and nothing, not even Charlie's opening his books and showing him his financial statements, prepared Bill for what they were to talk about. (190, p. 238)

Towns told Bill he had been watching him, and he wanted Bill to know he had the greatest respect for what he and the members of his group were doing. Would Bill like to move the entire operation to the hospital and make it his headquarters? Towns was prepared to give Wilson an office, a very decent drawing account, plus a healthy slice of the profits. Bill would be a lay therapist and Towns was positive that in no time at all Bill would be the most renowned and successful therapist in New York, the number-one man. (190, p. 238) Bill had not worked steady for seven years and this was the break he'd been looking for. His initial reaction was disbelief, followed by acceptance, and he said he would call Towns the next day with a definite answer.

Bill then called the members of his group to Clinton Street and informed them of the offer. He told them what a splendid fellow Towns was and promised them that Charlie Towns could be trusted. (190, p. 239) The group members were all negative toward the idea. They reminded Bill that there were to be no bosses in the group, that the only authority would be the group conscience and that all decisions were to be made by the group. This principle was something Bill and Dr. Smith had talked about from the beginning. Now he, Bill Wilson, was being asked to put this principle into practice. In the morning he phoned Charlie Towns and told him he couldn't accept the offer.

In August 1937, Bill Wilson and the unnamed group broke away from the Oxford Group. Bill felt that alcoholics had trouble with the rather aggressive evangelism of the Oxford Group. (199, p. 74)

By October 1937, the group had forty sober members split between Akron and New York. Two important concerns faced them: the financial situation of Dr. Bob Smith, and Bill's insistence that the group should use a book or pamphlets to spread their program instead of word of mouth.

In an effort to raise money Bill proposed paid missionaries and profit-making hospitals, but was summarily turned down. Bill spent the next six weeks trying to get contributions from "every rich man in Manhattan," without success. Angry and depressed, Wilson vented his spleen to his brother-in-law, Dr. Strong, in a "diatribe about the stinginess and shortsightedness of the rich." After listening to Bill, Strong remembered a girl he'd gone to school with, a niece of Willard Richardson, who worked for John D. Rockefeller, Jr. Richardson remembered Strong and set up an appointment with Rockefeller. The group requested $50,000. That request was denied, but $5,000 was placed in the treasury of the Riverside Church for their use. Three thousand dollars went to pay off Smith's mortgage and Wilson and Smith would receive thirty dollars each per week as long as the money held out. (190, pp. 254-255; 191, p. 57)

Bill started work on his book in May 1938, while the money drive was still on. A member of the group, Hank Parkhurst, made his secretary, Ruth Hock, available to Bill. As each chapter was completed, it was read and edited by the Clinton Street members, then sent to the Akron group for their opinions. (184, p. 111; 190, pp. 256-257) Meanwhile, the New York and Akron members started writing their stories for the book. A publishing company called Works Publishing Incorporated was proposed, with six hundred issues of stock, par value of $25. (Works Publishing Company actually incorporated June 30, 1940). Few shares were sold at first; group members considered the idea too foolhardy. The project was aided by Charlie Towns, who loaned them $2,500. The prospectus drawn up by Bill & Hank showed the estimated profits on sales of a million books. (199, p. 157)

As the book approached publication, a title was needed. Lois, in her biography, related the following:

> Thinking up titles for the book was a great game, and dozens were suggested, among them, "The Way Out," "Dry Frontiers," and "The Empty Glass." The New York group had labeled itself simply a nameless bunch of drunks, and this led one of the men, a former writer for the New Yorker Magazine, to dream up the title of "Alcoholics Anonymous." (184, pp. 114-115)

The book was published in April 1939, with a run of 4,730 copies. Sales were very slow, even with 20,000 postcards mailed to doctors and an ad in the

New York Times. Eventually, radio interviews and magazine articles generated many more sales.

Chapter Eight

WILLIAM GRIFFITH WILSON
1934-1939

The "Hot Flash"

Ebby Thatcher had visited Bill Wilson at the end of November 1934. Ebby brought with him a program of sobriety which he had learned from the Oxford Group. Prior to Bill's last detoxification Bill had also visited the Oxford Group which was headquartered at Sam Shoemaker's Calvary Church. Bill's failure to find any help from the Oxford Group precipitated what Wilson was later to describe as the worst binge of his drinking career. Putting away two to three quarts of gin per day for three days is the suggested amount that he drank. One must realize that if he was making this "bathtub gin," it usually had a lower alcoholic content than the standard 50%. (206)

The preceding chapter has outlined Wilson's mental and physical state prior to his admission at Towns Hospital December 11, 1934. Wilson's height varies between 6"1' and 6"3', depending on the source, with his average weight being 180 lbs. He may have been forty pounds underweight during his last drunk. He proceeded on that December day to Towns Hospital by himself.

The weather that day was a typical New York winter day with the temperature around 20 degrees farenheit, windy and cloudy. If Wilson took the subway then he would have walked some eight blocks along Clinton Avenue to the Borough Hall stop of the B'Way and 7th Avenue Subway. In mid-Manhattan he had to transfer at the Chambers-Hudson station to the 8th Avenue Subway Line. Exiting he then would have walked along Central Park West to Towns.

Towns believed that lack of occupation was the greatest destroyer of men and called them "vagrant types." His methods of helping an alcoholic were useless if, once detoxified, the man had no job to go back to. No one was admitted to Towns unless they paid in advance or had a "backer." The unemployed alcoholic was accepted under these monetary rules, but Towns considered these men as "preferred risks." (158, p. 104)

In a 1917 article, Towns had claimed that

> ... medical men have been largely responsible for making the alcoholic believe that alcoholism is a disease. The only extent to which a man can be alcoholically diseased is the extent to which he has been taking alcohol, in such quantities and with such regularity over a certain period of time that he has established a definite tolerance; and if he has been taking it in sufficient quantities, this tolerance would mean, in the end, that if he were suddenly deprived of his stimulant, delirium tremens and all of the unfavorable consequences that come out of that condition would result. (158, p. 103)

Isbell, et. al., thirty-eight years later, demonstrated clinically that Towns' hypothesis was correct. (207)

Towns also believed that one could not inherit a craving for drink, that an employer should take steps when an employee had lost control from the use of alcohol, and in the importance of educating children with "a campaign of enlightment." (158, p. 105) He also believed society, in one way or another, was wholly to blame for the alcohol problem and that society was directly responsible to those unfortunates who for any reason lost control of themselves from the use of alcohol. (208)

Upon Wilson's arrival at Towns Hospital, he was placed in a bed and the Towns-Lambert Treatment was begun. Dr. Lambert described the belladonna treatment as follows:

> Briefly stated, it consists in the hourly dosage of a mixture of belladonna, hyoscyamus and xanthoxylum. The mixture is given every hour, day and night, for about fifty hours. There is also given about every twelve hours a vigorous catharsis of C.C. pills and blue mass. At the end of the treatment, when it is evident that there are abundant bilious stools, castor oil is given to clean out thoroughly the intestinal tract. If you leave any of the ingredients out, the reaction of the cessation of desire is not as clear cut as when the three are mixed together. The amount necessary to give is judged by the physiologic action of the belladonna it contains. When the face becomes flushed, the throat dry, and the pupils of the eyes dilated, you must cut down your mixture or cease giving it altogether until these symptoms pass. You must, however, push this mixture until these symptoms appear, or you will not obtain a clear cut cessation of the desire for the narcotic . . . (17, p. 2126; 209, p. 186)

The exact contents of each ingredient is outlined below:

Belladonna Specific

Tincture belladonnae _____ 62. gm.
Fluidextracti xanthoryli.
Fluidextracti hyoscyami _____ .31 gm.
(210)

Belladona - Atropa belladonna

Deadly nightshade; a perennial herb with dark purple flowers and black berries. Leaves and root contain atropine and related alkaloids which are anticholinergic. It is a powerful excitant of the brain with side effects of delirium (wild and talkative), decreased secretion, and diplopia. (211, p. 112)

Xanthoxylum - Xanthoxylum Americanum

The dried bark or berries of prickly ash. Alkaloid of Hydrasts. Helps with chronic gastro-intestinal disturbances. Carminative and diaphoretic. (211, p. 269)

Hyoscyamus - Hyoskyamos

Henbane, hog's bean, insane root from the leaves and flowers of Hyoscyamus Niger. Contains two alkaloids, hyoscyamine and hyoscine. Nervous system sedative, anticholinergic, and antispasmodic. (211, p. 275)

Close observation is necessary in treating the alcoholic in regard to the symptoms of the intoxication of belladonna, as alcoholics are sensitive to the effects of belladonna delirium. According to Lambert, it is a less furious and less pugnacious delirium than that of alcohol. The patients are more persistent and more insistent in their ideas and more incisive in their speech concerning hallucinations. The hallucinations of alcohol are usually those of an occupation delirium; those of belladonna are not. The various hallucinations of alcohol follow each other so quickly that a man is busily occupied in observing them one after another. The belladonna delirium is apt to be confined to one or two ideas on which the patient is very insistent. If these symptoms of belladonna intoxication occur, of course, the specific must be discontinued; then beginning again with the original smaller dose. [210, pp. 987-988] Towns believed the attending physician would find it most difficult to differentiate between alcoholic delirium and belladonna delirium. [208, p. 7]

The vigorous catharsis of C.C. pills and blue mass are outlined below.

C.C. Pills

Extracti colocynthidis compositi	.08 gm.
Hydrargyri chloridi mitis	.06 gm.
Cambogiae	.016 gm.
Resinae jalapae	.02 gm.

These compound cathartic pills were used to help with perfect bowel elimination, characteristic of this were dark, thick, green mucous stools. [158, p. 8]

Blue Mass Pills - pilule catharticae vegetabilis

Extracti colocynthidis compositi	.06 gm.
Extracti hyoscyami	
Extracti jalapae	.03 gm.
Extracti leptandrae	
Extracti resinae podophylli	.015 gm.
Olei menthae piperitae	.008 gm.

When an alcoholic was admitted in the midst of his spree, or at the end of it, the first thing that was done was to put that patient to sleep, and the only medication which preceded his hypnotic was the four C.C. pills. The hypnotic which gave Lambert the best results was the following:

Chlorali hydrati	1. gm.
Morphinae	.008 gm.
Tincturae hyoscyami	2. gm.
Tincturae zingiberis	.6 gm.
Tincturae capsici	.3 gm.
Aquae ad	15. gm.

This could be given and the dose repeated in an hour, with or without one or two drachms of paraldehyde. If these were not effective within two hours, or even less, and the patient was of the furious, thrashing, motor type, a hypodermic injection of the following would almost invariably quiet him:

Strychminae sulphatis	.002 gm.
Hypseyamin sulphatis	.0006 gm.
Apomorphinae hydrochloridi	.006 gm.

(210, p. 988)

If the patient had been very hard to put to sleep and needed all these hypnotics, Lambert let him sleep until he awoke naturally before beginning the belladonna specific. If, however, he went to sleep easily with the chloral hydrate and paraldehyde, it was safe to wake him every hour for his specific, and he would quickly drop off to sleep. Lambert also believed it wise to give most alcoholics 1/60 to 1/30 of a gram of strychnine every four hours. In the young robust alcoholic, this may not be necessary, but in the majority of those at the end of a protracted spree it was more often indicated. Fourteen hours after the beginning of the belladonna specific, the patient was again given a cathartic. The older alcoholics and those in a weakened or poor physical condition would have with their milk one or two ounces of whiskey about four times a day. The whiskey and milk were usually not required after three days. The average patient would begin to show the characteristic green stool after the second dose of C.C. pills and blue mass, then an ounce of castor oil was given. (210, p. 988)

After this treatment, with its vigorous elimination, the patient would feel languid and relaxed, but the craving for alcohol would have ceased. For the next two or three nights, if they could not sleep, they were assisted with some hypnotic, such as trional, and they would be given, at regular intervals, any good vigorous tonic that would not contain alcohol, but that would act quickly. For at least a week following this treatment they would continue their tonic and live on a simple diet which could be easily digested, but they had an abundance of food.

Lambert believed his patients should be treated as individuals and not fall into the dangerous habit of routine treatment. He emphasized that this treatment was not an infallible cure for alcoholism, for there was no such cure, short of the grave. The treatment would obliterate the craving and establish a patient's self-confidence to go on without alcohol; it would do all that could be done for the man who honestly desired to be helped, but as sure as that man lived, and just as long as he lived, he could not touch alcohol in any form whatsoever without the danger of a relapse.

Bill Wilson's spiritual experience, or "hot flash," as he would call it, occurred during the second or third night (depending on the source) of the above treatment. Considering his alcohol and chloral hydrate [212] use upon entering Towns and adding this to the hypnotic drugs he received during the first few day of his stay, there is a possibility that his "hot flash" <u>may have been</u> delusions and hallucinations characteristic of momentary alcoholic toxic psychosis. [213; 214; 215]

William James in <u>The Varieties of Religious Experience</u> illustrates many cases of sudden conversion similar to the above interpretation, calling the types "anaesthetic revelations." [144, p. 379] It is unimportant what factors precipitate the conversion experience or "how it happens," only "what is attained." [14, p. 236] James also suggests that, "If the fruits for life of the state of conversion are good, we ought to idealize and venerate it," even if the specific cause is unclear. (144, p. 232)

It was the following day after his "experience" that Wilson read William James' The Varieties of Religious Experience (VRE) from "cover to cover." (199, p.64) Bill Wilson did admit that VRE was difficult reading at the time, but as the accounts of Wilson's experience relate, he did comprehend the meanings in VRE and would later incorporate them into the ideology of Alcoholics Anonymous. The section to follow will present a brief summary of William James and the book in question.

William James and The Varieties of Religious Experience

In a review of the Emmanuel and Oxford Groups' literature, William James' VRE is the most often quoted book. Wilson quoted James as saying that deflation at depth was necessary for a sudden conversion. The phrase 'deflation at depth' does not appear in VRE. (191, p.23) What James does say is that transforming spiritual experiences are nearly always founded on calamity and collapse. Conversion, as helping individuals, was discussed earlier in a previous chapter. What follows are various examples of conversion in VRE that pertain specifically to alcoholics:

1. The sway of alcohol over mankind is unquestionably due to its power to stimulate the mystical faculties of human nature, usually crushed to earth by the cold facts and dry criticisms of the sober hour. Sobriety

diminishes, discriminates, and says no; drunkenness expands, unites and says yes. (144, pp. 377-378)

2. S.H. Hadley's conversion is given a lengthy description. It is similar to that of Bill Wilson's. "Jesus, can you help me? I felt the glorious brightness of the noonday sun shine into my heart, I felt I was a free man. From that moment on I have never wanted a drink." (144, p. 199)

3. The conversion of temperance advocate, John B. Gough, is also illustrated, quoted by Leuba.

4. The conversion of the Oxford graduate is given the most attention by James. "I was willing. In such a surrender lies the secret of a holy life. From that hour drink has had no terrors for me." (144, pp. 218-219)

5. In the chapter on Saintliness, James suggests that the belief in a higher power is the fundamental feature in the spiritual life. (144, p. 269)

6. The only cure for "dipsomania" was "religiomania."

7. James, in several of his books including VRE, stressed the importance of "letting go" as both passive surrender and active sacrifice.

Many of the references to "alcohol" and "drunkenness" are found in the index of VRE. Although Bill Wilson did not cite these examples in his latter writings they probably reinforced his belief in the necessity for a spiritual experience in the "cure" for alcoholism.

Bill Wilson did have a spiritual experience at Towns Hospital, regardless of what were the "reasons" behind it. Sudden conversions happen less often than those of a gradual nature. Wilson stressed in latter writings that his type of conversion experience is not the only one that is rewarding to the alcoholic. Wilson cites James' "educational variety" which develop slowly over a period of time. Alcoholics Anonymous does not require a certain type of conversion experience for its members.

Kurtz in Not God suggests "Wilson's efforts over many years to give intellectual respectability to Alcoholics Anonymous sprang from his own deep need as well as from his perception of the needs of others." [191, p. 23] This statement refers to Wilson calling William James one of the founders of AA. The opinion of this writer differs from Kurtz. William James being given credit as a founder of AA was more of a fact related by Wilson than from some "deep need." The Emmanuel and Oxford Movement also cite the contribution of VRE to their beginnings and not because they needed to add "respectability" to their organization.

Another "founder" of AA in Wilson's opinion was Carl Jung who helped Rowland Hazard, who in turn helped Ebby who helped Wilson. There is a gap in Hazard's obituary for the period between 1927 and 1935. These are also the dates when he said that he had visited Dr. Jung in Zurich. It is impossible to obtain patient records from this period and Hazard's name was not found in a search of Jung's written works. [217]

The Varieties of Religious Experiences was published in 1902 and translated into German in 1907. James and Jung met each other September 19, 1909 and spent two evenings together. [218, p. 265] These meetings took place at an international congress at Clark University in New York honoring Stanley Hall, its president, as well as the twentieth anniversary of the university. James went there primarily to hear Sigmund Freud deliver a speech. (219, p. 122) What Jung may have said to Hazard, after his treatment failure with Jung's techniques, was that the alcoholic is sometimes helped by a spiritual experience. Jung was familiar with James' ideas and also probably had read VRE in the German edition. In Jung's book Psychological Types, much attention is given to James' philosophy. An investigation on the part of Bill Wilson into Jungian psycho-therapy took place during the 1940s when Wilson was under the psychiatric care of Dr. Tiebout for his depression.

Until his death, Bill Wilson maintained the importance of Carl Jung to the founding of Alcoholics Anonymous. He wrote Jung in January 1961, some twenty-seven years after he declared Jung a founder of AA. Jung was 86 years old when he received Wilson's letter and in ill-health. In April, he suffered a stroke and stayed comatose until he died in June 1961, five months after Wilson's letter. Jung spent his last years in the mountains of Kusnacht, Switzerland and his home contained none of his client records. Jung did indicate in his Analytical Psychology that he often sent alcoholic patients to the Oxford Group.

The following section discusses the Oxford Group and the reasons why the "alcoholics" left the group.

The Oxford Group

There is little doubt about the Oxford Group's contributions in influencing the formation of Alcoholics Anonymous. One of the preceding chapters dealt with Frank Buchman and the "Groupers" and is sufficient to an understanding of their principles, history and methods. Two of the reasons this author found significant factors in causing the break with the Oxford Group are first, the comments by Frank Buchman praising Adolf Hitler and his visits with Himmler (176, p. 77) and second, that Catholic Cannon Law forbade Catholics from joining other religious groups and many of the early members of Alcoholics Anonymous were Catholic (over 50% of the members in Akron, for example). (221; 222) Blumberg summarizes the reason for the split as follows:

> Bill W. and his associates came from diverse backgrounds and their discussions in the early days were fraught with controversy. One way to resolve controversy and to head off divisiveness was to limit the focus of the group to alcoholism; thus participants could differ on theology and politics and the group would not be threatened. Bill W. and his associates thereby incorporated the pluralist approach to social and moral reform that was common to the United States of their day - to attract a diversity of members and interested followers on the basis of a single purpose.

The often-cited idea that the Oxford Group did not approve of alcoholics as members and that this was also a factor in the split does not hold up upon examination.

The Oxford Group's expansive literature can be traced to the writings of Harold Begbie. In 1909 he wrote <u>Twice-Born Men</u>, which contains studies in the regeneration (conversion) of human beings. This book was dedicated to William James and the first section of the book outlined James' <u>The Varieties of Religious Experience</u>. The several editions of <u>Twice-Born Men</u> sold 500,000 copies and "William James was so moved by its narratives that he said his own book, <u>The Varieties of Religious Experience</u>, might well be a postscript to it." (175, d.j.) The 1927 Begbie book <u>Life Changers (More Twice-Born Men)</u> is devoted to Frank Buchman exclusively. Other Begbie books include stories of the saving of alcoholics through conversion.

Wilson, speaking of Sam Shoemaker in 1955, related the following:

> It was from Sam Shoemaker that we absorbed most of the Twelve Steps of Alcoholics Anonymous, steps that express the heart of AA's way of life. Sam Shoemaker had given us the concrete knowledge of what we could do about it, he passed on the spiritual keys by which we were liberated. The early AA got its ideas of self-examination, acknowledgement of character defects, restitution for harm done, and working with others straight from the Oxford Group and directly from Sam Shoemaker, their former leader in America, and from nowhere else. (199, p.39)

Beginning with the publication of <u>Realizing Religion</u> in 1921, Shoemaker wrote nine other books prior to the AA's publication of <u>Alcoholics Anonymous</u> in 1939 (appendix C). These books deal primarily with redemption through conversion. The most important contribution of these works was that in his writings Shoemaker made continuous reference to Samuel McComb's work at Emmanuel Church in Boston, <u>The Varieties of Religious Experience</u>, and Jerry McAuley's Water Street Mission.

Three books published during the 1930s by Oxford Group members are devoted entirely to accounts of their lives as active alcoholics and their sobriety through Group membership. These books are <u>The Big Bender</u>, <u>I Was a Pagan</u>, and <u>Life Began Yesterday</u> (appendix D). These books are very similar in style to the accounts found in the story section of <u>Alcoholics Anonymous</u>. Appendix D also includes a list of other story-type books about the Oxford Group in the 1930s. These books are not necessarily about alcoholics, but they do give personal accounts of how the Oxford Group helped these individuals.

One characteristic of most group movements is that one book is referred to as the "Bible" of that organization. In the case of the Oxford Group, the book that acquired that distinction was <u>For Sinners Only</u> by Arthur James Russell.

> This book by A.J. Russell, one of London's newspaper editors, describes his pilgrimage as a prodigal into the Oxford Group. The book has had a very wide sale in England, and the religious movement with which it deals is making noticeable headway in the United States. The group meets at "house parties," and the idea is, broadly, that each person's own conscience shall be his preacher. It was such house parties that Mr. Russell attended, and his interest, at first objective, became introspective also. As an observer, he became a convert.

This <u>New York Times</u> book reviews concludes, "It is obvious that a final judgment on this kind of volume is not to be passed by any reviewer or newspaper. It is for the reader himself to decide what he thinks of Mr. Russell's narratives." (223)

Russell believed that all pretensions, professional and material success, and political or social prestige fell short of making people genuinely happy. He argued that an evangelism was thus no less needed in the 1930s as in biblical times. Harry Hadley, the son of Samuel Hopkins Hadley, is mentioned by Russell. S.H. Hadley, who ran Jerry McAuley's Water Street Mission cited above, was one of William James' prime examples of how conversion can help a drunkard find abstinence. Harry Hadley went to work for Sam Shoemaker at Calvary Church. William James, <u>VRE</u>, alcoholics, Sam Shoemaker and Sam's conversion are also cited by Russell.

Russell concluded his book with the following remarks:

> The Oxford Group showed me in practice what I knew in precept: that "the heart must be at leisure from itself"; that to share is better than to preach; to lose is really to find; to "let go" is to be held secure; to surrender all is to possess all things. (178, p. 292)

An interesting aside is another book written by A.J. Russell in 1932 called <u>God Calling</u>. This book contains daily inspirational readings. <u>God Calling</u> was used as an outline for Richmond Walker as he wrote a book of daily inspirational readings for alcoholics, <u>24-Hours a Day</u>. Walker offered his book to Bill Wilson and AA in 1950 for them to publish. After the General Service Conference refused the offer, Pat Butler, representing The Hazelden Foundation of Center City, Minnesota, acquired the rights to publish 24-Hours a Day. To date this small volume has sold over 4 million copies. Not only did the writings of A.J. Russell have an impact on the early AA member, but it also has influenced alcoholics through Hazelden's publication of 24-Hours a Day.

The positive literature of the Oxford Group is extensive but a few books can be found criticizing the Group (appendix E). Saints Run Mad by Marjorie Harrison gives a detailed outline of the dangers of the Oxford Group. She writes: "... one of the most important facets of the Oxford Group is the insistence upon a definite conversion that can be pinned down to some specified time, place, and emotional condition, rather than upon the slow building-up of the religious life on a completely unemotional basis." (224, p. 18) Harrison was critical of Groupers showing a lack of humility as they always tried to appeal to the wealthy, their use of planchettes, their lovingly relentless pursuit for members, their sanction of independent thinking, and their tired testimonials (which were taught and expected to be humorous). "Such unfortunates as Oxford members are gullible to the preaching of Buchman." (224, p. 83)

Whether the books were pro or con toward the Oxford Group, the early members of the yet unnamed fellowship had a wide variety of reading material to choose from. The books read by Bill Wilson can only be speculated on, but he did, in 1941, acknowledge the influence of the oral and written teachings of the Oxford Group, especially Sam Shoemaker, on the ideas of AA.

The writing of the book, <u>Alcoholics Anonymous</u> has been discussed previously using the "official" version of the endeavor, but the section which follows will provide additional information regarding that undertaking.

Writing of the "Big Book"

The first edition of <u>Alcoholics Anonymous</u> had a publication run of approximately 5,000 copies. The reason that edition of the book and its subsequent printings are referred to as the "Big Book" is that the paper stock initially used was unusually thick. The second printing was thinner and colored blue, instead of red cloth, as in the first printing. Also, a red and yellow dust jacket was added to the printings of the first edition, sometimes called the "circus" dust jacket. The second and third editions have blue dust jackets.

Wilson began the book by dictating his ideas to his typist, Ruth Hock. Bill, chain-smoking, would pace back and forth expounding his ideas. At various intervals he would include his philosophizing off the subject using lengthy, flowery metaphors that would later be edited out. [216; 225] His writings [190, p. 257], as they became chapters, were read and edited by the other members in New York and then sent to Dr. Bob. He also edited chapters along with members from the Akron Group and Cleveland Groups. Bill felt he was more of an "umpire" than an author. (190, p. 263)

Following the idea of Shoemaker (226, p. 103), Wilson believed that a section of personal stories should be added to the text. As stories were being written in New York, Akron was having trouble with getting members to finish their stories by the publication deadline. Dr. Bob found a drunk named Jim down on the Akron skid-row who had been a newspaperman. Bob put him in the hospital to dry out and told Jim that if he could straighten out he could help the members on their stories. "Jim did sober up, and helped the Akron and Cleveland men with their stories and made rewrites, but he was careful to keep the same flavor." (220, p. 154)

The chapter entitled "To Wives" was written by Bill following the same rewriting process. Wilson had asked Dr. Bob's wife to write the chapter, but she declined. Lois did not write the chapter, either - she was not asked. Lois had expected to write the chapter "To Wives" and also "The Family Afterwards." (184, p. 114) "I've always been hurt by it, and I still don't know why Bill didn't ask me," she later wrote. (220, p. 152)

Perhaps the greatest display of opposition against Bill Wilson's efforts came during the selection of the title for the book. Bill half jokingly wanted to call the book, "The William Wilson

Movement," and sign his name as author. (184, p. 114; 190, p. 264) The final chapter in the first edition is called "The Lone Endeavor." It deals with an alcoholic sobering up by using the "Big Book" alone with no other members around. A pre-publication multilith copy of the "Big Book" had been sent to a young man, who wrote back that he had sobered up out west by reading the book. (227, p. 395) This chapter was deleted from the second printing because they lost contact with the young man. The chapter "Lone Endeavor" was not written by Bill, but surprisingly by his typist, Ruth. (216)

Prior to the printing of the "Big Book" in April of 1939, the entire manuscript was given to Tom Uzzel, an accomplished magazine editor and teacher of short story writing at New York University. The first edition of the "Big Book" contained 400 pages. Tom Uzzel had to edit out 800 pages to reach that length. (216; 227) The "grudge list," used in all editions of the "Big Book" as the explanation of the Fourth Step in the chapter "How It Works," is a variation of the game of "truth" taught by the members of the Oxford Group. (228, p. 89)

Located in the Archives of Alcoholics Anonymous in New York City (Box 31, Folder 19.2) are titles of readings that Bill Wilson and early AAs found helpful. (191, p. 256; 229) The following discussion will deal with these books.

Books Early AAs Found Helpful

According to Nell Wing, former secretary to Bill Wilson during the years 1950 - 1971 and the General Service office archivist from 1971 to 1982, there were at least ten books that were read by Bill Wilson and others between 1935 and 1939 that were helpful to them. Three of these books have previously been given detailed accounts in this paper. They are Richard Peabody's <u>The Common Sense of Drinking</u>, A.J. Russell's <u>For Sinners Only</u>, and William James' <u>The Varieties of Religious Experience</u>.

The other titles on the list (appendix B) deal primarily with the power of prayer, biblical teachings, and first century Christianity. Two of the books on the list were by Glenn Clark who was a professor of English at Macalaster College in St. Paul, Minnesota and a prolific writer. In addition to the titles on the list, "all his books were popular with the early AAs." (229)

The presence of Peabody's <u>The Common Sense of Drinking</u>, as a book read by early AAs, has implications beyond the fact that it is the only text on alcoholism cited on the list. It also brings the Emmanuel Movement into relationship with Alcoholics Anonymous.

Dr. Bob Smith added to the list of books that helped him and other members in Akron and Cleveland. It appears that those members relied on the Bible more than the New York members did. Inspirational passages from the Bible and other books that were "required" reading under Dr. Bob's leadership can be found in appendix F. (220, p. 96)

In researching this paper other books should be added to the list of those that influenced Bill Wilson. According to Lois Wilson, she and Bill frequently read <u>My Utmost for His Highest</u> by Oswald Chambers. This book contains daily inspirational readings which cover all phases of Christian life and service. Bill read Beverly Nichols' <u>The Fool Hath Said</u> over and over, which discusses the Oxford Group and the teachings of Christ as they apply to twentieth century life. (230; 231)

Chapter Nine

SUMMARY, CONCLUSIONS, AND RECOMMENDATIONS

Summary

This study has assessed the use of alcohol and alcoholism in an historical perspective up until the publication of the book, Alcoholics Anonymous. Emphasis has been placed on the etiology, classification, and treatment of alcoholics during the period of the 1890s.

More detail has been given to the period that followed, 1900-1939. Charles B. Towns, the Emmanuel Movement, Peabodyism, and the Oxford Group were discussed. The life of Bill Wilson, up to 1939, has been given lengthy attention. The writing of the "Big Book" has also been covered.

From what has been written thus far, there appears to be many sources that influenced Bill Wilson. The intention of this author has been to write a volume of interest not solely to the academic community. The members of Alcoholics Anonymous, perhaps whose knowledge of alcoholism begins in 1939, could possibly benefit from this reading. A knowledge of the past indicates to this author the effectiveness of AA, as it incorporates helpful ideas that have been used in past history. One is also reminded that Bill Wilson did not wish to be known as a saint, a prophet, an author, or the inventor of a new religion, but as just another alcoholic trying to stay sober one day at a time.

Conclusions

After Prohibition, the interest in helping alcoholics was almost non-existent. The rise of the "Welfare State" during the thirties brought alcoholism once again under the auspices of the medical profession. For whatever reasons, whether grandiosity, complete ignorance of others, at this time, the medical establishment ignored the work of pre-Prohibition doctors and their investigations of alcoholism. By 1934, the medical establishment was again calling alcoholism a disease and the alcoholic sick, instead of bad, which was nothing new to students of the pre-1919 disease concept.

Adolph Meyer, Psychiatrist-in-Chief at Johns Hopkins, predicted the rise of a self-help group in the treatment of alcoholism in 1932. (206, p. 299) This may have been realized by Lambert also, who pushed Silkworth into guiding Bill Wilson. Silkworth's allergy ideas came directly from his training under Lambert at Bellevue. Lambert was familiar with the Quarterly Journal of Inebriety, which spoke of an allergy as early as 1876.

The connection between AA and the Laboratory of Applied Physiology of Yale (later moved to Rutgers) is often cited as beginning with Wilson's visit to the Yale School of Alcohol Studies in 1944. However, Wilson may have contacted

Norman Jolliffe and Mark Keller of the Laboratory in 1938, in response to Jolliffe's article on the use of vitamins in treating alcoholics. (233)

Bill Wilson had first gone to Sam Shoemaker's Calvary Church Mission in November 1934 and although physical proximity does not mean acquaintance, one wonders if possibly Wilson and/or Shoemaker knew Richard Peabody. Nell Wing does remember Bill Wilson saying he did meet Peabody. When Richard Peabody died suddenly on april 27, 1935 of a heart attack, at the age of 43, his residence was 24 Gramercy Park, NYC. Also, Shoemaker was familiar with the Emmanuel Movement. With Peabody's death, his concepts and treatment of alcoholism left New York City to be continued in Philadelphia under Chambers and Strecker.

The "fit" between the individuals in this study can be seen in the following chart. My conclusion, based on the above data, is that Sam Shoemaker and the Oxford Group were the pivotal and most influential ingredients in the founding, and formation of AA, and the publication of <u>Alcoholics Anonymous</u>.

Summary, Conclusions, & Recommendations   187

Figure 2
Chronological Chart of Precursors to AA

                        Jerry McAuley

      E.D. Starbuck   J.H. Leuba

Keeley

                  S.H. Hadley

    Samuel McComb   William James   Harold Begbie

Towns

    Emmanuel Movement

Lambert   Jacoby Club

                                    Frank Buchman
                                    Oxford Group

    Courtenay Baylor

    Elwood Worcester H. Hadley

Silkworth

      R.R. Peabody   Sam Shoemaker   A.J. Russell
                     William G. Wilson

                   Alcoholics Anonymous

                                      <u>God Calling</u>
                                  Richmond Walker
                                        Pat Butler
                         Hazelden
                                    <u>24-Hours A Day</u>

Recommendations

In light of the above conclusions of this study, a number of recommendations are warranted.

Members of Alcoholics Anonymous, this study suggests, may benefit from knowledge of the precursors of their movement. Bill Wilson, who was schooled in Scientific Temperance Instruction, had lived through the propaganda of the anti-saloon movement, Prohibition, and the reframing of alcoholism as a sickness assurging responsibility away from the person.

I agree with the idea posited by Mark Lender, that we, in the "alcoholism movement" and the members of Alcoholics Anonymous, are temperance workers. According to Lender,

> In the context of their times, they have tried to alleviate drinking problems, to increase public awareness of this area, and (with the exception of AA, which endorses no political or social programs), to influence the formulation of relevant public policy. The old temperance movement did nothing less in its era. [234, p. 188]

Yes, we are all products of our past; therefore, the present treatment of alcoholics may benefit by a more detailed explanation of the past prior to the 1930s.

The editions of the "Big Book" do not mention meeting attendance as vital to sobriety. Entering alcoholism treatment, in- or out-patient, and attending meetings do not a conversion make. Sobriety, through membership in Alcoholics

Summary, Conclusions, & Recommendations 189

Anonymous, is best maintained when one works with active alcoholics. The well-intentioned efforts of the "Treatment Industry" to help active alcoholics has taken the key ingredient of keeping its members abstinent (12th Step) partially away from Alcoholics Anonymous.

It is hoped that the interested reader will discern additional areas for inquiry from this study. It is further anticipated that future investigations will examine many of the other relevant issues, such as the implications of alcoholism and drug abuse for those who begin their usage during a period when that usage is illegal, as was the case for Bill Wilson himself, and for many individuals in the 1960s when marijuana and other hallucinogenic substances were first popularly introduced into our culture, and is still the situation facing many adolescents today.

Appendix A
References Suggested in Peabody's Book

<u>Outline of Abnormal Psychology</u>, Professor William McDougall.

<u>Intelligent Living</u>, Dr. Austen Fox Riggs.

<u>The Structure and Meaning of Psychoanalysis</u>, Healy, Bronner, and Bowers.

<u>The Human Mind</u>, Dr. Karl A. Menninger.

<u>Why We Misbehave</u>, Dr. Samuel D. Schmalhausen.

<u>The Foundations of Personality</u>, Dr. Abraham Myerson.

<u>A General Introduction to Psychoanalysis</u>, Professor Sigmund Freud.

<u>Psychoneurosis and Psychotherapy</u>, Professor J. Dejering and Dr. E. Gaukler (translated by Dr. S.E. Jelliffe).

<u>Progressive Relaxation</u>, Dr. Edmund Jacobson.

<u>Remaking a Man</u>, Courtenay Baylor.

<u>The Human Machine</u>, Arnold Bennett.

<u>How to Live on 24 Hours a Day</u>, Arnold Bennett.

<u>Diseases of the Nervous System</u>, Dr. S.E. Jelliffe and Dr. W.A. White.

<u>The Beloved Ego</u>, Dr. Wilhelm Stekel.

Appendix A (continued)

<u>Understanding Human Nature</u>, Dr. Alfred Adler.

<u>Habits</u>, William James.

<u>Psychoanalysis For Normal People</u>, Geraldine Coster.

Appendix B
Nell Wing's List of "Books Early AAs Read

Allen, James. *As a Man Thinketh.*

Browne, Lewis. *This Believing World.*

Browne, Lewis. *The Conversion Experience.*

Clark, Glenn. *I Will Lift Up Mine Eyes.*

Clark, Glenn. *This Changing World.*

Fox, Emmet. *The Sermon on the Mount.*

James, William. *The Varieties of Religious Experience.*

Peabody, R.R. *The Common Sense of Drinking.*

Russell, A.J. *For Sinners Only.*

Troward, Thomas. *The Edinburgh Lectures on Mental Science.*

Appendix C
Sam Shoemaker Books

Realizing Religion	1921
Children of the Second Birth	1927
Religion That Works	1928
Twice Born Ministers	1929
If I Be Lifted Up	1931
A Confident Faith	1932
The Conversion of the Church	1933
The Gospel According to You	1934
National Awakening	1936
The Church Can Save the World	1938

Harold Begbie Books

Twice-Born Men	1909
Souls in Action	1911
The Ordinary Man	1915
Life Changers	1927

Appendix D
Books Written by Oxford Group Members

Allen, G. He That Cometh.

Allen, G. Tell John.

Brown, P.M. The Venture of Belief.

Browne, A. Sowers and Seekers.

Chambers, O. My Utmost For His Highest.

Clapp, C. The Big Bender.

Crothers, R. Susan and God.

DuMaurier, D. Come Wind, Come Weather.

Foot, S. Life Began Yesterday.

Goodspeed, E.J. The Strange New Gospels.

Grensted, L.W. Person of Christ.

Jones, O. Inspired Children.

Jones, O. Inspired Youth.

Kitchen, V.C. I Was a Pagan.

Landau, R. God Is My Adventure.

Macaulay, R. Going Abroad.

Macmillian, E. Seeking and Finding.

MacMillian, E. Finding and Following.

Appendix D   (continued)

McKenney, R. Industrial Valley.

Nichols, B. The Fool Hath Said.

Pfatteicher, E.P. The Man From Oxford.

Raynor, F. The Finger of God.

Redwood, H. Kingdom Come.

Redwood, H. The Quiet Quest.

Reynolds, A.S. New Lives for Old.

Rose, C. When Man Listens.

Rose, H. The Quiet Time.

Russell, A.J. For Sinners Only.

Russell, A.J. One Thing I Know.

St. Denis, R. An Unfinished Life.

Sangster, W.E. God Does Guide Us.

Viney, H. How Do I Begin?

Walter, H.A. Soul Surgery.

Winslow, J.C. Why I Believe.

Winslow, J.C. Church in Action.

Appendix E
Books Critical of Oxford Group

Bennett, J.C. <u>Social Salvation</u>.

Braden, C.S. <u>These Also Believe</u>.

Ferguson, C.W. <u>The Confusion of Tongues</u>.

Harrison, M. <u>Saints Run Mad</u>.

Henson, H.H. <u>The Oxford Group Movement</u>.

Macintosh, D.C. <u>Personal Religion</u>.

Richardson, J.A. <u>The Group's Movement.</u>

Appendix F
Dr. Bob's Required Reading List

<u>The Holy Bible</u>, King James Version.

> The Sermon on the Mount
> The Lord's Prayer
> The Book of James
> The 13th Chapter of First Corinthians

<u>The Upper Room</u> (Methodist periodical).

<u>The Greatest Thing in the World</u>,
Henry Drummond.

<u>The Varieties of Religious Experience</u>,
William James.

<u>For Sinners Only</u>, A.J. Russell.

APPENDIX G
The AA Preamble, Steps and Traditions

The A.A. Preamble (1947)

Alcoholics Anonymous is a fellowship of men and women who share their experience, strength and hope with each other that they may solve their common problem and help others to recover from alcoholism.

The only requirement for membership is an honest desire to stop drinking. A.A. has no dues or fees. It is not allied with any sect, denomination, politics, organization or institution. Does not wish to engage in any controversy. Neither endorses nor opposes any cause. Our primary purpose is to stay sober and help other alcoholics to achieve sobriety.

The A.A. Preamble (1958 to present)

Alcoholics Anonymous is a fellowship of men and women who share their experience, strength and hope with each other that they may solve their common problem and help others to recover from alcoholism.

The only requirement for membership is a desire to stop drinking. There are no dues or fees for A.A. membership; we are self-supporting through our own contributions. A.A. is not allied with any sect, denomination, politics, organization or institution; does not wish to engage in any controversy, neither endorses nor opposes any causes. Our primary purpose is to stay sober and help other alcoholics to achieve sobriety.

Reprinted with permission of The A.A. Grapevine, Inc.

The Steps (1938)

1. We admitted that we were licked, that we were powerless over alcohol.
2. We made a moral inventory of our defects or sins.
3. We confessed or shared our shortcomings with another person in confidence.
4. We made restitution to all those we had harmed by our drinking.
5. We tried to help other alcoholics, with no thought of reward in money or prestige.
6. We prayed to whatever God we thought there was for power to practice these steps.

The Twelve Steps (1939 Multilith)

1. Admitted we were powerless over alcohol - that our lives had become unmanageable.
2. Came to believe that a Power greater than ourselves could restore us to sanity.

3. Made a decision to turn our will and our lives over to the care and direction of God as we understand him.

4. Made a searching and fearless moral inventory of ourselves.

5. Admitted to God, to ourselves, and to another human being the exact nature of our wrongs.

6. Were entirely willing that God remove all these defects of character.

7. Humbly, on our knees, asked Him to remove our shortcomings - holding nothing back.

8. Made a list of all persons we had harmed, and became willing to make complete amends to them all.

9. Made direct amends to such people wherever possible, except when to do so would injure them or others.

10. Continued to take personal inventory and when we were wrong promptly admitted it.

11. Sought through prayer and meditation to improve our contact with God, praying only for knowledge of His will for us and the power to carry that out.

12. Having had a spiritual experience as the result of this course of action, we tried to carry this message to others, especially alcoholics, and to practice these principles in all our affairs.

The Twelve Steps (Publication of Big Book (1939) to present)

1. We admitted we were powerless over alcohol - that our lives had become unmanageable.

2. Came to believe that a Power greater than ourselves could restore us to sanity.

3. Made a decision to turn our will and our lives over to the care of God <u>as we understand Him</u>.

4. Made a searching and fearless moral inventory of ourselves.

5. Admitted to God, to ourselves, and to another human being the exact nature of our wrongs.

6. Were entirely ready to have God remove all these defects of character.

7. Humbly asked Him to remove our shortcomings.

8. Made a list of all persons we had harmed, and became willing to make amends to them all.

9. Made direct amends to such people wherever possible, except when to do so would injure them or others.

10. Continued to take personal inventory and when we were wrong promptly admitted it.

11. Sought through prayer and meditation to improve our conscious contact with God <u>as we</u>

<u>understand Him</u>, praying only for knowledge of His will for us and the power to carry that out.

12. Having had a spiritual awakening as the result of these Steps, we tried to carry this message to alcoholics, and practice these principles in all our affairs.

The Twelve Traditions

1. Our common welfare should come first; personal recovery depends on A.A. unity.

2. For our group purpose there is but one ultimate authority - a loving God as He may express himself in our group conscience. Our leaders are but trusted servants; they do not govern.

3. The only requirement for A.A. membership is a desire to stop drinking.

4. Each group should be autonomous except in matters affecting other groups or A.A. as a whole.

5. Each group has but one primary purpose - to carry its message to the alcoholic who still suffers.

6. An A.A. group ought never endorse, finance, or lend the A.A. name to any related facility or outside enterprise, lest problems of money, property, and prestige divert us from our primary purpose.

7. Every A.A. group ought to be fully self-supporting, declining outside contributions.

8. Alcoholics Anonymous should remain forever non-professional, but our service centers may employ special workers.

9. A.A., as such, ought never be organized; but we may create service boards or committees directly responsible to those they serve.

10. Alcoholics Anonymous has no opinion on outside issues; hence the A.A. name ought never be drawn into public controversy.

11. Our public relations policy is based on attraction rather than promotion; we need always maintain personal anonymity at the level of press, radio, and films.

12. Anonymity is the spiritual foundation of our Traditions, ever reminding us to place principles before personalities.

A Declaration of Unity

This we owe to A.A.'s future:

> To place our common welfare first;
> To keep our fellowship united.
> For on A.A. unity depend our lives,
> And the lives of those to come.

I Am Responsible...

> When anyone, anywhere, reaches out for help, I want the hand of A.A. always to be there. And for that: I am responsible.

Reprinted by permission of Alcoholics Anonymous World Services, Inc.

APPENDIX H
Additional Information for AA and Al-Anon

The A.A. Grapevine, Inc.
PO Box 1980
Grand Central Station
New York, NY 10163

A.A. General Service Office
PO Box 459
Grand Central Station
New York, NY 10163

Al-Anon Family Group Headquarters
PO Box 862
Midtown Station
New York, NY 10018

LIST OF REFERENCES

1. Brown, W.L. Inebriety and its "cures" among the Ancients. Quart. J. Inebr., 1898, 20:125-141.

2. Seneca. Epistle LXXXIII: On drunkenness. Classics of the alcohol literature. Quarterly Journal of Studies on Alcohol, 1942, 3:302-307.

3. Macfie, C. History of prohibitive legislation. Quarterly Journal of Inebriety, 1900, 22:52-57.

4. Rolleston, J.D. Alcoholism in classical antiquity. British Journal of Inebriety, 1927, 24:101-120.

5. Keller, M. A Historical Overview of Alcohol and Alcoholism. Cancer Research, 1979, 39:2822-2829.

6. Kerr, N. Wines, Scriptural and Ecclesiastical. London: J & A Churchill & Co., 1881.

7. Dorchester, D. The Liquor Problem In All Ages. New York: Phillips & Hunt, 1887, 26-28.

8. Rolleston, J.D. Alcoholism in Mediaeval England. British Journal of Inebriety, 1934, 31:33-49.

9. Keller, M. and McCormick, M. A Dictionary of Words About Alcohol. New Brunswick, New Jersey: Journal of Studies on Alcohol, Incorporated, 1968.

10. Levine, H.G. The Discovery of Addiction. Journal of Studies on Alcohol, 1978, 39(1):143-154.

11. Krout, J.A. The Origins of Prohibition. New York: Knopf, 1925, 63-90.

12. Mann, M. Primer on Alcoholism. New York: Rinehart & Co., Inc., 1950.

13. Myerson, D.J. The Study and Treatment of Alcoholism. New England Journal of Medicine, 1957, 257:820-825.

14. Gusfield, J.R. Symbolic Crusade. Urbana: University of Illinois Press, 1963.

15. Austin, G.A. Perspectives on the History of Psychoactive Substance Use. Rockland, Maryland: National Institute on Drug Abuse, 1978.

16. Corwin, E.H.L. and Cunningham, E.V. Institutional Facilities for the Treatment of Alcoholism. Quarterly Journal of Studies of Alcoholism, 1944, 5:9-85

17. Blumberg, L. The Ideology of a Therapeutic Social Movement: Alcoholics Anonymous. Journal of Studies on Alcohol, 1977, 38(11):2122-2143.

18. Maxwell, M.A. The Washingtonian Movement. <u>Quarterly Journal of Studies on Alcoholism</u>, 1950, 11:410-451.

19. Douglas, C.J. Historical Notes on the Sanitorium Treatment of Alcoholism. <u>Medical Rec.</u>, 1900, 57:410-411.

20. Lender, M.E. and Karnchanapee, K.R. Temperance Tales. <u>Journal of Studies on Alcoholism</u>, 1977, 38(7): 1347-1370.

21. Debove. Alcohol ed Alcoolismo. <u>La Riforma Med.</u>, 1898, 4:733-735.

22. Crothers, T.D. <u>Diseases of Inebriety</u>. Hartford, Conn.: n.p., 1893.

23. Bacon, S.D. The Classic Temperance Movement of the U.S.A.: Impact of Today on Attitudes, Action, and Research. <u>British Journal of Addiction</u>, 1967, 62:5-18.

24. Blocher. Impotanza delle Societa Anti-alcooliche. <u>La Riforma Med.</u>, 1897, 4:118.

25. Forel, A. The Therapy of Alcoholism. <u>Medical Record</u>, 1888, 34:712.

26. Centennial Temperance Conference. <u>One Hundred Years of Temperance: A Memorial Volume</u>. Philadelphia, Pennsylvania: NTS Publ. House, 1885, 123-141.

27. Parrish, J. <u>Alcoholic Inebriety: From a Medical Standpoint</u>. Philadelphia, Pennsylvania: P. Blakenston, Son & Co., 1883, 75-88.

28. Palmer, C.F. <u>Inebriety its Source, Prevention and Cure</u>. Philadelphia, Pennsylvania: The Union Press, 1898, 30.

29. Wilkins, D. <u>The Curse of The World Narcotics: Why Used: What Effects: The Remedy</u>. Chicago, Illinois: Blakely Printing Co., 1887, 343-347.

30. Parke, M.J. Dipsomania. <u>Cleveland Journal of Medicine</u>, 1898, 3:484-488.

31. Arthur, T.S. <u>Strong Drink: The Curse and the Cure</u>. San Francisco, Calif.: Hubbard Brothers, 1877, 443-446.

32. Manning, F.N. The Immediate and Ultimate Treatment of the Inebriate. <u>Australasian Medical Gazette</u>, 1899, 18:221-225.

33. Wilson, G.R. The Mismanagement of Drunkards. <u>Journal of Mental Science</u>, 1898, 44:411-429.

34. Reid, G.A. The Temperance Fallacy. <u>Lancet</u>, 1899, 2:1006-1012.

35. Comby. L'Alcool Nellapractica Infantile. <u>Morgagni</u>, 1897, 39(2):298-300.

36. Hare, F. <u>On Alcoholism</u>. London: J & A Churchill Co., 1912.

37. Crivelli, M. Alcoholism, its Pathological Physiology and its Treatment. Intercolonial Med. J., 1900, 5:48.

38. Alcoholism and its Effects in Paris. Med. Rec., 1887, 32:582.

39. Lentz. Discussion Sur L'Alcoolisme. Acad. Royale Belgique Bull., 1897, 11:156-180.

40. Jewett, C. Speeches, Poems, and Miscellaneous Writings on Subjects Connected with Temperance and the Liquor Traffic. Boston: J.P. Jewett, 1849, 9-25.

41. Montgomery, H. The Way Out. New York: Hunt & Eaton, 1895.

42. Blair, H.W. The Temperance Movement or The Conflict Between Man and Alcohol. Boston: Wm. E. Smythe Co., 1888.

43. Beard, G.M. Causes of the Recent Increase of Inebriety in America. The Quarterly Journal of Inebriety, 1876, 1(1):38.

44. Avait, M.H. La Question des establissments Speciaux pour la Cure de l'Alcoolisme. Bull. Gen. de Therap., 1900, 140:28-29.

45. Mosel, J. Prevention of Mental Disease. Sanit., 1900, 44:99-113.

46. Cutten, G.B. The Psychology of Alcoholism. New York: Scribner's & Sons, 1907.

47. Forel, A. La Question des Asiles our Alcoolises Incurables. Rev. Med. de la Suisse Romande, 1899, 19:522-535.

48. Rolleston, J.D. Auguste Forel and His Campaign Against Alcohol. Brit. J. Ineb., 1939, 36:43-60.

49. Gordon, E. The Anti-Alcohol Movement in Europe. New York: F.H. Revell Co., 1913.

50. Staples, H.L. Alcoholism. Northwest Lancet, 1899, 19:121-127.

51. Pickett, D. ed. The Cyclopedia of Temperance Prohibition and Public Morals. New York City: The Methodist Book Concern, 1917 edition.

52. Crothers, T.D. Inebriety and its Symptomology. Quarterly Journal of Inebriety, 1878, 2:193-198.

53. Benedict, A.L. The Treatment of Inebriety. Retrosp. of Med., 1898, 117:197-198.

54. Gallavardin, M. The Homeopathic Treatment of Alcoholism. Philadelphia: Hahnemann Publishing House, 1890.

55. Wilcox, H.H. On the Wane. Albert Lea Med. J., 1898, 1:94-95.

56. Kynett, H.H. Medical Temperance. Med. Surg. Reporter, 1897, 75:51-52.

57. Crothers, T.D. Reformed Men as Asylum Managers. Quart. J. Inebr., 1897, 19:79.

58. Pitcairn, J.J. Prison Treatment of Alcoholics in England. Quart. J. Inebriety, 1897, 19:142-151.

59. Pitcairn, J.J. Inebriety and the Penal Law in Europe and in the United States. Quart. J. Inebr., 1897, 19:329-343.

60. Pitcairn, J.J. Alcoholism and the Penal Law. Med. Surg. Reporter, 1897, 75:362.

61. Forgue, E. Pourquoi et Comment il Faut Combattre l'Alcoolisme? Nouv. Mont Pellier. Med. 9, 1899, 2:358-377.

62. de Montyel, E.M. La Therapeutique de l'Alcoolisme par l'Internement Prolonge des Buveurs. Rev. de Med., 1897, 17:23-49.

63. de Montyel, E.M. La Therapeutique de l'Alcoolisme. Revue Neurol., 1897, 5:516-517.

64. Jean, R. L'Organisation de la Lutte Contre l'Alcoolisme. Rev. Hyg. Med. Soc., 1956, 4:748-761.

65. Curatel. Process. Quart. J. Inebr., 1897, 19:99.

66. Lucas-Championniere, J. L'Alcoolisme en Allemange. J.de Med., 1897, 68:559-560.

67. Lucas-Championniere, J. Des Causes de L'Alcoolisme et des Moyens de la Combattre. <u>J. de Med.</u>, 1897, 68:49- 55.

68. Courtois-Suffet. Les Grandes Intoxications. <u>Arch. Gen. de Med.</u>, 1898, 2:608-609.

69. Courtois-Suffet. Les Grandes Intoxications, l'Al coolisme. <u>Arch. Gen. de Med.</u>, 1899, 2:545-614.

70. Rosebrugh, A.M. Probation and Treatment of Inebriates. <u>Canad. Pract.</u>, 1900, 25:392-394.

71. Barella. Discussion sur l'Alcoolisme. <u>Acad. Royale de Belgique Bull.</u>, 1897, 11:853-964.

72. Soltau, H.K.V. The Scope and Effect of Institutional Treatment of Alcoholism. <u>Brit. J. Addic.</u>, 1948, 51:15-19.

73. Cery. Editorial. <u>Med. News</u>, 1900, 76:575-576.

74. de Martines, C. De Quelques Traitements de l'Alcoolisme et de Celui employe a l'Asile de Cery. <u>Rev. Med. de la Suisse Romande</u>, 1900, 20:128-135.

75. St. Blennorragie. Alcoolisme. <u>Lyon Med.</u>, 1887, 93:582.

76. Forel, A. Terapia dell'Alcoolisme Cronics e della Dipsomania. <u>La Riforma Med.</u>, 1897, 4:104.

77. Oberdieck, F. Beitrage Zurkenntniss des Alkoholismus und Seiner Ratio-Nellen Behandlung. Rivista di Patol. Nerv. Ement., 1897, 2:430.

78. Chatelain. L'Asile de POntareuse pour la Guerisson des Buveurs. Ann. Medico-Psych., 1899, 10:64-76.

79. Kerr, N. Progress for the Movement for Compulsory Curative Treatment for Habitual Drunkards in Britain. Quart. J. Inebr., 1897, 19:111-122.

80. Wallers, A.R. Report of Lady Henry Somerset's Industrial Farm Colony for Inebriates. Lancet., 1898, 1:909.

81. Kerr, N. What Shall We Do With Alcoholic Inebriates and Others Apparently Insane. Medico-Legal J., 1897, 14:1- 6.

82. Partridge, G.E. Studies in the Psychology of Intemperance. New York: Sturgis & Walton, 1912.

83. Kerr, N. Inebriety, and How it Can be Cured. Quart. J. Inebriety, 1886, 8:84-87.

84. Rosebrugh, A.M. The Treatment of Inebriates. Canad. Pract., 1898, 23:311-314.

85. Rosebrugh, A.M. The Treatment of Inebriates. Quart. J. Inebriety, 1898, 20:279-288.

List of References

86. Rosebrugh, A.M. The Treatment of Inebriates. Quart. J. Inebriety, 1898, 20:409-415.

87. Crothers, J.D. Classification and Asylum Treatment of Chronic Alcoholism. Med. Rec., 1900, 58:1024-1025.

88. Crothers, T.D. The Curability of Inebriety by Medical Treatment. Miss. Valley Med. Assoc. Trans., 1900, 2:354-365.

89. Turner, J.E. The History of First Inebriate Asylum in the World. New York: n.p., 1888.

90. Bargy, F. De L'Alcoolisme ou Point de Vue de la Prophylaxie et du Traitement. La Presse Med. 6, 1898, 1:68.

91. Brower, D.R. Treatment of Alcoholism. Med. Stand., 1899, 22:352-353.

92. Cooper, J.W.A. The Treatment of Inebriety by Psycho-therapy. Brit. J. Inebriety, 1911, 8:135-142.

93. Crothers, T.D. Clinical Treatment of Inebriety. Quart. J. Inebriety, 1902, 24:129-147.

94. Crivelli, M. The Treatment of Alcoholism. Lancet, 1900, 1:1473.

95. Davis, N.S. Some Considerations of Alcoholism and its Treatment. Quart. J. Inebriety, 1897, 23:94-104.

96. McMichael, G.H. Some Thoughts on Alcoholism. Med. Rec., 1897, 51:839-840.

97. Atwell, C. Anti-alcoholic Serum in france. Sanit., 1900, 45:348-349.

98. Forel, A. The Alcohol Question. Amer. J. Insanity, 1900, 57:297-317.

99. Burrall, F.A. The Treatment of Alcoholism by Suggestion. J.A.M.A., 1897, 28:399-400.

100. Mason, O. Forms of Suggestion Useful in the Treatment of Inebriety. Quart. J. Inebriety, 1897, 19:219-225.

101. Quakenbos, J.D. The Treatment of the Drink Habit by Hypnotic Suggestion. Med. Rec., 1900, 58:1025-1027.

102. Sinani, B. Du Role de la Suggestion dans la Lutte Contre Alcoolisme. Rev. Neuro., 1900, 8:131-132.

103. Sparks, A. Alcoholism in Women -- its Cause, Consequence, and Cure. Med. Rec., 1898, 52:699-701.

104. Rybakow. Hypnotism in the Treatment of Alcoholics. Vratch., 1898, 18:517-579.

105. Bramwell, J.M. Dipsomania and its Treatment by Suggestion. Quart. J. Inebriety, 1900, 22:293-298.

106. Bramwell, J.M. On the Treatment of Dipsomania and Chronic Alcoholism by Hypnotic Suggestion. Quart. J. Inebriety, 1903, 25:122.

107. Kelley, L.E. The Non-Heredity of Inebriety. Chicago: S.C. Griggs & Co., 1896.

108. Cherrington, E.H., Johnson, W.E., Porter, A., Stoddard, C.F., eds. Standard Encyclopedia of the Alcohol Problem, Vol. VI. Westerville, Ohio:; American Issue, 1930.

109. Daniels, W.H. The Temperance Reform and Its Great Reformers. New York: Nelson & Phillips, 1878.

110. A Member of the Society. The Foundation, Progress and Principles of the Washingtonian Temperance Society of Baltimore. Baltimore: John D. Toy, 1842.

111. Merceir. The Treatment of Chronic Alcoholism With Strychnine. NY Med. J., 1897, 66:307.

112. Federoff. Strychnine in Alcoholism. Therap. Gazette, 1898, 22:766.

113. Hammond, G.M. Alcoholism. Internat. Med. Ann., 1897, 18:69.

114. Combemale, F. Alcoholism, Strychnine in Chronic Care. Retro. of Med., 1897, 116:43.

115. Wallace, J.R. Six Cases of Alcoholism Treated Success fully by Inhibition of Alcohol, Massage, and Bromides. Dublin J., 1899, 108:443.

116. Treatment of Alcoholism. Med. Stand., 1897, 19:336-338.

117. Wilson, G.R. Drunkenness. New York: Scribners, 1893.

118. Jacobson, D.E. On Patogenesen of Delirium Tremens. Hospitalstid, 1897, 40:141-156.

119. Savage, G.H. Alcholic Insanity. Guys Hospt. Gaze., 1899, 13:353-362.

120. Baudry, J.K. Results of Treatment in 1,129 Cases of Acute Alcoholism. Quart. J. Inebriety, 1900, 22:58-67.

121. Masbrenier, J. Traitement du Delirium Tremens par les Injections sous Cutanus de Serum Artificiel. Rivista di Patrol. Nerv. Ementale., 1900, 5:48.

122. Hidden, C.W. The Treatment of Alcoholism. Med. World, 1900, 18:277-278.

123. Douglas, C.J. Treatment of Alcoholism. New York Med. J., 1899, 70:626-628.

124. Gentles, H.W. The Pathology and Treatment of Chronic Alcoholics. Quart. J. Inebriety, 1897, 19:393-399.

List of References

125. Hall. New Methods of Treatment for Inebriety. Quart. J. Inebriety, 1898, 20:119-120.

126. Chatier, M.E. Logical Treatment of Alcoholism. Med. Brief 28, 1900, 1:1816-1817.

127. Hickling, D.P. Treatment of Delirium Tremens. Virginia Med., Semi-month., 1900, 5:199-203.

128. Robinson, M.W. The Immunological Properties of Alcohol. Ann. of Allergy, 1950, 8:468-487.

129. Broca-Soucellier, Sepalier, and Thibault. Anti-ethyline. Sanit., 1900, 44:234.

130. Legrain. La Cure des Buveurs Apropos de Serum Antialcooliques. Arch. de Neurol., 1900, 2:50-52.

131. Evelyn, F.M. New Methods of Treatment for Inebriety. Quart. J. Inebriety, 1898, 20:119-120.

132. Apple Cure. Med. Brief, 28, 1900, 1:20.

133. Food Cures. In New Methods of Treatment for Inebriety. Quart. J. Inebriety, 1898, 20:119-120.

134. Vine, G. The Prevention of Alcoholism. Lancet., 1898, 2:1125.

135. Gonorrhea, a Cure for Inebriety. <u>Canad. Pract.</u>, 1900, 25:170.

136. Plankegarde. In New Methods of Treatment for Inebriety. <u>Quart. J. Inebriety</u>, 1898, 20:119-120.

137. American Medical Association. <u>Nostrums and Quackery</u>. Chicago: A.M.A. Press, 1905.

138. Brander, N.R. Empiric and Charlatan Efforts to Cure Inebriates. <u>Quart. J. Inebriety</u>, 1897, 19:270-277.

139. Gold-cures and Other Cures. <u>Cleveland J. Med.</u>, 1898, 3:499-500.

140. Crothers, T.D. Gold Cures in Inebriety. <u>J.A.M.A.</u>, 1898, 31:755-757.

141. Cherrington, E.H., Johnson, W.E., Porter, A., Stoddard, C.F., eds. <u>Standard Encyclopedia of the Alcohol Problem</u>, Vol. IV. Westerville, Ohio: American Issue, 1928.

142. Starbuck, E.D. <u>The Psychology of Religion</u>. New York: Scribners, 1903.

143. Peabody, F.G. <u>Jesus Christ and the Social Question</u>. New York: MacMillian & Co., 1900.

144. James, W. <u>The Varieties of Religious Experience</u>. New York: Modern Library, 1936. (orig. 1902).

List of References

145. Leuba, J.H. A Study in the Psychology of Religious Phenomena. J. of Psy., 1896, 7(3):309-385.

146. Cherrington, E.H., Porter, A., Johnson, W.E., Stoddard, E.F., eds. Standard Encyclopedia of the Alcohol Problem, Vol. III. Westerville, Ohio: American Issue, 1926.

147. Chapman, J.W. S.H. Hadley of Water Street. New York: Fleming Revell Co., 1906.

148. Offord, R.M. Jerry McAuley - An Apostle to the Lost. New York: American Tract Society, 1907.

149. Shoemaker, H.S. I Stand by the Door. New York: Harper & Row Pub., 1967.

150. Odegard, P.H. Pressure Politics. New York: Columbia University Press, 1928.

151. Baron, S. Brewed in America: A History of Beer and Ale in the United States. Boston: Little, Brown and Company, 1962.

152. Paredes, A. The History of the Concept of Alcoholism. In R.E. Tarter and A.A. Sugerman, Alcoholism. Reading, Massachusetts: Addison-Wesley Publishing Company, 1976.

153. Chidsey, D.B. On and Off the Wagon. New York: Cowles Book Company, 1969.

154. Jolliffe, N. The Alcoholic Admissions to Bellevue Hospital. Science, 1936, 83(2152):306-309.

155. Musto, D.F. The American Disease. New Haven: Yale University Press, 1973.

156. MacFarlane, P.C. The "White Hope" for Drug Victims. Colliers, November 29, 1913, 16-17; 29-30.

157. Towns, C.B. Drug and Alcohol Sickness. New York:; M.M. Barbour Company, 1932.

158. Towns, C.B. The Sociological Aspect of the Treatment of Alcoholism. The Modern Hospital, 1917, 8:103-106.

159. Worcester, E., McComb, S., Coriat, I. Religion and Medicine: The Moral Control of Nervous Disorders. New York: Moffat, Yard & Co., 1908.

160. McCarthy, R.G. Alcoholism: Attitudes and Attacks, 1775- 1935. In S.C. Bacon, ed. The Annals: Understanding Alcoholism. Philadelphia: The American Academy of Political and Social Science, 1958.

161. MacDonald, R. Mind, Religion and Health. New York: Funk and Wagnalls Company, 1909.

162. Baylor, C. Remaking A Man. New York: Moffat, Yard & Company, 1919.

163. Mann, M. <u>Marty Mann Answers Your Questions About Drinking and Alcoholism</u>. New York: Holt, Rinehbart & Winston, 1970.

164. Anderson, D. <u>The Other Side of the Bottle</u>. Wyn, New York: H.W. Wilson Co., 1950.

165. Bowman, K.M. and Jellinek, E.M. Effects of Alcohol on the Individual. In E.M. Jellinek, ed. <u>Alcohol Addiction and Chronic Alcoholism</u>, Vol. 1. New Haven: Yale University Press, 1942.

166. Anderson, D. The Place of the Lay Therapist in the Treatment of Alcoholics. <u>Quarterly Journal of Studies on Alcohol</u>, Sept. 1944, 2:157-266.

167. Peabody, R.R. Psychotherapy for Alcoholics. <u>New England Journal of Medicine</u>, 1930, 202:1195-1202.

168. Peabody, R.R. Psychotherapeutic Procedure in the Treatment of Chronic Alcoholism. <u>Mental Hygiene</u>, 1930, XIV:109-128.

169. Peabody, R.R. Psychotherapeutic Treatment of Inebriates. <u>The British Journal of Inebriety</u>. July 1930, 28(1):55- 60.

170. Peabody, R.R. <u>The Common Sense of Drinking</u>. Boston: Little, Brown and Company, 1930.

171. Worcester, E. *Body, Mind and Spirit*. Boston: Marshall Jones Company, 1931.

172. Strecker, E. and Chambers, F. *Alcohol - One Man's Meat*. New York: The MacMillian Company, 1938.

173. Bishop, J. *The Glass Crutch*. New York: Doubleday, Doran & Co., Inc., 1945.

174. Murray, R.H. *Group Movements Throughout the Ages*. London: Hodder and Stroughton Limited, 1935.

175. Begbie, H. *Life Changers (More Twice-Born Men)*. New York: G.P. Putnam's Sons, 1927.

176. Clark, W.H. *The Oxford Group, Its History and Significance*. New York:; Bookman Associates, 1951.

177. Shoemaker, S.M. *Children of The Second Birth*. New York: Fleming H. Revell Company, 1927.

178. Russell, A.J. *For Sinners Only*. New York:; Harper & Brothers Publishers, 1932.

179. Van Dusen, H.P. An Apostle to the Twentieth Century. *Atlantic Monthly*, July 1934, 1-16.

180. Roots, J.M. An Apostle to Youth. *Atlantic Monthly*, December 1928, 807-817.

181. <u>Oxford Group International Party</u>, June 23-July 29, 1934. Oxford: The Oxford Group, 1937. (pamphlet).

182. <u>March of Events</u>. Oxford: Oxford University Press, 1935. (pamphlet).

183. <u>New Witness</u>. Montreal, vols. 1,2,3, July 1936 to February 1938. (weekly).

184. Al-Anon Family Group. <u>Lois Remembers</u>. Don Mills, Canada: ; T.H. Best Printing Company, 1979.

185. Winslow, J.C. <u>Why I Believe in the Oxford Group</u>. London: Hodder and Stoughton, 1934.

186. Eister, A.W. <u>Drawing-Room Conversion</u>. Durham, North Carolina: ; Duke University Press, 1950.

187. Buchman, F.N.D. <u>Remaking the World</u>. New York: McBride & Company, 1949.

188. Cantril, H. <u>The Psychology of Social Movements</u>. New York: John Wiley and Sons, Inc., 1941.

189. Reynolds, P.D. <u>A Primer in Theory Construction</u>. Indianapolis: Bobbs-Merrill Co., Inc., 1977.

190. Thomsen, R. <u>Bill W.</u> New York: Harper & Row, Publishers, 1975.

191. Kurtz, E. Not-God: A History of Alcoholics Anonymous. Center City, MN: Hazelden Educational Services, 1979.

192. Thompson, Z. Vermont. Burlington: Z. Thompson, publisher, Chauncey Goodrich, printers, 1848.

193. Haywood, J. The New England Gazetteer. Boston: Boyd & White, 1839.

194. Morrissey, C.T. Vermont - A History. New York: W.W. Norton & Company, Inc., 1981.

195. Webster's Biographical Dictionary. Springfield, Massachusetts: G & C Merriam Company, 1980.

196. Cherrington, E.H., Johnson, W.E., Porter, A., Stoddard, C.F., eds. Standard Encyclopedia of the Alcohol Problem, Vol. II. Westerville, Ohio: American Issue, 1924.

197. Information Please Almanac. New York: A & W Publisher, Inc., 1983. 37th edition.

198. The New York Times, November 26, 1895, XLV(13, 811).

199. Alcoholics Anonymous Comes of Age. New York: Alcoholics Anonymous World Services, Inc., 1979. 8th printing.

200. Brecker, E.M. Licit and Illicit Drugs. Boston: Little, Brown and Company. Publisher's Review Copy, 1972.

201. Steele, J.D. <u>Hygienic Physiology and Alcoholic Drinks and Narcotics</u>. New York: American Book Company, 1901.

202. <u>Alcoholics Anonymous</u>. New York: ; Works Publishing Company, 6th printing, June 1944. 1st edition.

203. Harris, I. <u>The Breeze of the Spirit</u>. New York: The Seabury Press, 1978.

204. <u>The New York Times</u>, December 11, 1934.

205. <u>Bill W. 1895-1971</u>. New York: The Alcoholics Anonymous Grapevine, Inc., March 1971.

206. Emerson, H., ed. <u>Alcohol and Man</u>. New York: The MacMillian Company, 1932.

207. Isbell, H., et al. An Experimental Study of the Etiology of 'Rum Fits' and Delirium Tremens. <u>Quart. J. Stud. Alcohol.</u>, 1955, 16:1-33.

208. Towns, C.B. Successful Medical Treatment in Chronic Alcoholism. <u>The Modern Hospital</u>, 1917, 8:6-10.

209. Lambert, A. Care and Control of the Alcoholic. <u>Boston Med. Surg. J.</u>, 1912, 166:615-621.

210. Lambert, A. The Obliteration of the Craving for Narcotics. <u>Journal of the A.M.A.</u>, 1909, LIII(13):985- 989.

211. Hare, H.A. <u>Practical Therapeutics</u>. New York: Lea Bros. & Co., 1904. 10th edition.

212. Wilson, W.G. Those Goof Balls. New York: The Alcoholics Anonymous Grapevine, Inc., November 1945.

213. Johnson, J. M.D. Personal Interview, Ramsey County Medical Center, St. Paul, MN, May 23, 1981.

214. Carlson, J. Pharm. D. Personal Interview, University of Minnesota, Minneapolis, MN, May 21, 1981.

215. Harrison, et al. <u>Principles of Internal Medicine</u>. New York: McGraw-Hill, 1974. 7th edition.

216. Crecelius, Ruth Hock. Telephone Interview, July 12, 1982.

217. Albrecht, Doris B. Librarian, Kristine Mann Library. Analytical Psychology Club of New York, Inc., C.G. Center. Written Correspondence, June 9, 1982.

218. Van der Post, L. <u>Jung and the Story of Our Time</u>. New York: Random House, 1975.

219. Perry, R.B. <u>The Thought and Character of William James</u>. Westport, Connecticut: Greenwood Press, 1935 original, 1974 reprint Vol. II.

220. <u>Dr. Bob and the Good Oldtimers</u>. New York: Alcoholics Anonymous World Services, Inc., 1980.

221. Snyder, C. An Original Akron AA Member. Written Correspondence, October 22, 1981.

222. Caukwell, D. Rev. Personal Interview. University of Minnesota, Minneapolis, MN, February 8, 1983.

223. Russell, A.J. For Sinners Only. <u>The New York Times Book Review</u>, January 15, 1933.

224. Harrison, M. <u>Saints Run Mad</u>. London: John Lane and the Bodley Head Ltd., 1934.

225. Crecelius, Ruth Hock. Written Correspondence, December 5, 1981.

226. Ferguson, C.W. <u>The Confusion of Tongues</u>. Garden City, NJ: Doubleday, 1929.

227. Crecelius, Ruth Hock. Telephone Interview, January 28, 1983.

228. Kitchen, V.C. <u>I Was a Pagan</u>. New York: Haprer & Brothers, 1934.

229. Wing, Nell. Personal Interview. AA Archives, New York, New York, July 1, 1981.

230. Wilson, Lois. Written Correspondence, October 20, 1981.

231. Wilson, Lois. Personal Interview, Al Anon Convention, Minneapolis, MN, September 4, 1982.

232. Haggard, H.W. Critique of the Concept of the Allergic Nature of Alcohol Addiction. <u>Quart. J. Studies on Alcohol</u>, 1944, 5:233-241.

233. Keller, Mark. Personal Interview, Rutgers University, New Brunswick, NJ, July 7, 1981.

234. Lender, M.E. <u>Drinking in America</u>. New York: The Free Press, 1982.

235. Wilson, W.G. <u>Vitamin B-3 Therapy</u>. Phoenix, Ariz.: Do It Now Foundation, 1968.

236. Lender, M. Jellinek's Typology of Alcoholism. <u>J. Studies on Alcohol, 1976, 40(5):361-375.</u>

INDEX

A

Adams, John 5
Adler 110
Alcohol consumption 1, 7, 9-10, 17, 20, 24, 53
Alcoholics Anonymous 8, 87, 112, 136, 157, 160, 170
                                           172-176, 179, 181-182
American Temperance Society 7
American Association for the Study
   and Care of Inebriety 11, 22
American Society for the
   Promotion of Temperance 7, 55
Anti-Saloon League 55, 57, 82, 87, 116, 146
Archbishop of Canterbury 3
Arthur, T.S. 8, 79
Arsenic 58-59
Asylums 31-32, 34-40, 42, 49, 51, 64
Austria 29-30, 45
Avait, Marie 19-20, 37-38

B

Bacchanalian 1
Baylor, Courtenay 94-101, 112
Begbie, Harold 115
Beecher, Lyman 7, 137
Belladonna 152, 164-166, 168
Benezet, Anthony 5
Bible 2-3, 81, 117, 124

Binghamton 4, 26
Boniface, St. 3
Boston 49, 87-88, 101, 139, 146, 176
Boylan Bill 86
Buchman, Dr. Frank N.D. 113, 127, 174-175, 178
Burr and Burton Academy 135, 142-143, 151

C

Canada 10, 46, 64
Cery Retreat 36
Chambers 112
Chaucer 4
Chatelain 41-42
China 86, 117-118
Chloral hydrate 37, 61
Christians 2, 44, 89
Clark University 72, 173
Cocaine 87
Common Sense of Drinking, The 101, 182
Conversion 26, 72-80, 116, 121, 128, 155
                             169, 170-172, 175, 177-178
Coriat, Isador H., M.D. 88, 109
Cornell, Shep 151
Courts 29-30, 32, 43, 47
Crothers, T.D. 19, 22-24, 33-34, 37, 39, 40-41
                             43, 46-48, 52, 63, 65-66
Cruikshank, George 8

Index

D

Delirium tremens 8, 21, 32, 36, 39, 43, 48, 59, 70
151, 163, 165-166
Denial 96
Denmark 30, 120
Depression 92, 95, 109, 142, 144-145
147, 151-153, 173
Dipsomania 22-25, 33-34, 50, 52, 54, 57
62, 65-66, 72, 102

E

Eddy, Mary Baker 150
Eddy, Sherwood 117
Eighteenth Amendment 83
Elixirs 67, 146
Emmanuel Movement 87-91, 93, 100-101
109-112, 170, 172,182
Environment 12, 14, 16-17, 22, 25, 41
69, 75, 90, 104
Epileptics 20-21, 24, 31, 39, 42, 145
Etiology 11, 16-17, 31
Evangelical Protestant 87
Evangelistic Temperance 78-79

F

Fechner, Theodor 110
Federalist 6-7
First-century Christianity 90-91, 112, 116, 120, 182
Food cures 63
Ford, Henry 127

Forel 19-20, 29, 37, 39-41, 51
Forgue 28
Four Absolutes 118, 125
France 10, 15, 17, 19, 25, 28, 37
                                             51, 57, 61, 131
Franciscan 121
Franklin, Benjamin 5
Freud 110, 173

G

Galen 1
Genetics 14, 20
Germany 10, 19-20, 26, 29, 34-35, 57, 63
Gildas, St. 3
Gold cures 36, 67-69, 72
Gonorrhea 67
Gospel Temperance 78-79
Gospels of Christ 90
Gothenburg 30
Gower 4
Greeks 1-2
Guidance 106, 113, 117-118, 122-123, 125-126

H

Hadley II, Henry Harrison 80-81
Hadley, Samuel H. 80-81
Harrison Act 86
Hazard, Rowland 154
Heredity (cause of alcoholism) 11-14, 16, 39, 66, 90
House party 117, 120, 123-125

Index

Hungary 30
Huxley 110
Hypnotic treatment 26, 49, 51-54, 88, 90, 93, 105

I

Ireland 17, 80
Italy 10, 15, 17, 25

J

James I 4
James, William 72, 75, 88, 90-91, 107, 110-111
Jesus 110
Jewish 17
John the Baptist 3
Jung 110, 172-173

K

Kerr 41, 43-44, 46, 65
Keeley (gold cure) 36, 68-69
Keeley Institute 36, 44, 68-70
Keswick Convention 114, 116
Koran 2

L

Lambert, Dr. Alexander 85, 110, 157, 164, 166-169
Langland 4
Leuba, James H. 72, 75-76, 78-79
Lincoln Legion 55
Lord's Prayer 125

M

Mann, Marty	94
MacDonald, Robert	91, 93
Marijuana	58, 60, 87
Mather, Cotton	5
Mather, Increase	5
McComb, Rev.	88, 109-110, 176
McAuley, Jerry	80
McAuley's Water Street Mission	80, 176-177
Methodist	121-122
Middle Ages	4
Minnesota	120
Montanist	121
Moody, D.L.	79
"Moral-suasion effort"	78
Morphine	26, 60, 68, 70, 84, 110, 167
Morse, Jedidiah	7
Murphy, Francis	55

N

Nation, Carrie	57
New Testament	3, 91
Newman's Oxford Movement	113
Norwich University	135, 144-145

O

"Open" witness meeting	123, 126, 129
Opium	60, 71, 84, 86, 140
Oxford Group	90, 151, 153, 155-159

P

Palmer, Charles	63
Peabody, F.G.	74
Peabodyism	87-88, 101-107, 109, 111-112, 182
Pietistic	122
Pilgrims	5
Pliny	1, 2
Populists	57
Portugal	30
Prayer	37, 56, 78, 182
Prohibition	3, 27, 33, 55, 82-83, 87, 111, 133, 140, 146, 150

Q

Quack cures	26, 36, 51, 67-70, 87
Quarterly Journal of Inebriety, The	49, 83
Quiet time	123-125, 127-128

R

Rechabites	3
Restitution	116-117, 175
Romans, 1	2
Roosevelt, Theodore	85
Rush, Benjamin	6
Russia	29-30, 53

S

Samson	3
Sargent's, L.M.	8

Saxon 3
Scriptures 2
Seneca 2
Serum 26, 51, 61-62
Sharing 116, 122, 129, 177
Shoemaker, Samuel M. 81, 117, 151, 155, 157
                                    162, 175-177, 179-180
Slip 108
Soper's, T.N. 8
"Soul surgery" 127
Spain 30
Starbuck, Edwin Diller 72, 79
Sterilization 32, 62, 65, 66
Stockbridge, Massachusetts 120
Strecker 112
Strong, Dr. Leonard 148, 151, 159
Strychnine 58-59, 68-69, 72
Sunday, William "Billy" 79
Sutton, Thomas 8
Sweden 10, 30

T

Taft, President 82
Temperance Movement 3, 7-8, 55, 82
Ten Nights in a Barroom 8
Thatcher, Ebby 151-157, 162, 172
Towns, Charles B. 83-87, 110, 157-160, 164
Towns' Hospital 81, 150, 152, 155, 157
                                    162-166, 169, 171
Trotter, Dr. Thomas 6

Turks 2
Turner, Dr. Joseph 9
Treatment for alcoholism 1, 2, 5, 8-9, 11-15
20-22, 26-81, 164, 168-169, 173

V

Varieties of Religious Experience, The 75, 196-172
175-176, 182

W

WCTU 55
Washington Movement 8
Washington Total Abstinence Society 9
Webb-Kenyon Bill 82
Wesley, John 121-122
Whalon, Mark 141-142
Willard, Frances 140
Wilson, William Griffith 17, 31, 44, 59, 81
129, 131-183
Woe to Drunkards 5
Women's Christian Temperance Union 134, 140
Worcester, Rev. Elwood 88-89, 91, 94, 109-111
World War I, ...101, 145-146
Wundt, Wilhelm 110

Y

YMCA, ...116-117, 143
Yale Plan Clinics 94

Distributed by . . .

Hazelden Publishing & Educational Services
P.O. Box 176
15251 Pleasant Valley Road
Center City, MN 55012-0176

 HAZELDEN®

For price and order information, or a free catalog, please call
our Telephone Representatives.

1-800-328-9000
(Toll Free. U.S., Canada, and the Virgin Islands)

1-651-213-4000
(Outside the U.S. and Canada)

1-651-213-4590
(24-Hour FAX)

http://www.hazelden.org